Workbook v3.0

Brought to you by the Bootstrap team:

- Emmanuel Schanzer
- Kathi Fisler
- Shriram Krishnamurthi
- Dorai Sitaram
- Joe Politz
- Ben Lerner
- Flannery Denny
- Rachel Tabak

Visual Designer: Colleen Murphy

Computing Needs All Voices!

The pioneers pictured below are featured in our Computing Needs All Voices lesson. To learn more about them and their contributions, visit https://bit.ly/bootstrap-pioneers.

We are in the process of expanding our collection of pioneers. If there's someone else whose work inspires you, please let us know at https://bit.ly/pioneer-suggestion.

Notice and Wonder

Write down what you notice and wonder from the **What Most Schools Don't Teach** video.

"Notices" should be statements, not questions. What stood out to you? What do you remember? "Wonders" are questions.

What do you Notice?	What do you Wonder?

Windows and Mirrors

Think about the images and stories you've just encountered. Identify something(s) that served as a mirror for you, connecting you with your own identity and experience of the world. Write about who or what you connected with and why.

_____

_____

_____

_____

_____

_____

_____

_____

_____

_____

Identify something(s) from the film or the posters that served as a window for you, giving you insight into other people's experiences or expanding your thinking in some way.

_____

_____

_____

_____

_____

_____

_____

_____

_____

_____

Reflection: Problem Solving Advantages of Diverse Teams

This reflection is designed to follow reading LA Times Perspective: A solution to tech's lingering diversity problem? Try thinking about ketchup

1) The author argues that tech companies with diverse teams have an advantage. Why?

_____

_____

_____

_____

2) What suggestions did the article offer for tech companies looking to diversify their teams?

_____

_____

_____

_____

3) What is one thing of interest to you in the author's bio?

_____

_____

_____

_____

4) Think of a time when you had an idea that felt out of the box. Did you share your idea? Why or why not?

_____

_____

_____

_____

5) Can you think of a time when someone else had a strategy or idea that you would never have thought of, but was interesting to you and/or pushed your thinking to a new level?

_____

_____

_____

_____

6) Based on your experience of exceptions to mainstream assumptions, propose another pair of questions that could be used in place of "Where do you keep your ketchup?" and "What would you reach for instead?".

_____

_____

_____

_____

The Math Inside video games

- video games are all about *change!* How fast is this character moving? How does the score change if the player collects a coin? Where on the screen should we draw a castle?

- We can break down a game into parts, and figure out which parts change and which ones stay the same. For example:
  - Computers use **coordinates** to position a character on the screen. These coordinates specify how far from the left (x-coordinate) and the bottom (y-coordinate) a character should be. Negative values can be used to "hide" a character, by positioning them somewhere off the screen.
  - When a character moves, those coordinates change by some amount. When the score goes up or down, it *also* changes by some amount.

- From the computer's point of view, the whole game is just a bunch of numbers that are changing according to some equations. We might not be able to see those equations, but we can definitely see the effect they have when a character jumps on a mushroom, flies on a dragon, or mines for rocks!

- Modern video games are *incredibly* complex, costing millions of dollars and several years to make, and relying on hundreds of programmers and digital artists to build them. But building even a simple game can give us a good idea of how the complex ones work!

Notice and Wonder

Write down what you notice and wonder about the Ninja Cat Game.

"Notices" should be statements, not questions. What stood out to you? What do you remember?

What do you Notice?	What do you Wonder?

Reverse Engineer a video game

What is changing in the game? The first example is filled in for you.

(0, 480)   (640, 480)

(0, 0)   (640, 0)

Thing in the Game	What Changes About It?	More Specifically?
Dog	Position	x-coordinate

The coordinates for the PLAYER (NinjaCat) are: (_____ , _____)
                                                        x   y

The coordinates for the DANGER (Dog) are: (_____ , _____)
                                                    x   y

The coordinates for the TARGET (Ruby) are: (_____ , _____)
                                                     x   y

Brainstorm Your Own Game

Created by: _____

Background

Our game takes place: _____
In space? The desert? A mall?

Player

The Player is a _____

The Player moves only up and down.

Target

Your Player GAINS points when they hit The Target.

The Target is a _____

The Target moves only to the left or right.

Danger

Your Player LOSES points when they hit The Danger.

The Danger is a _____

The Danger moves only to the left or right.

Artwork/Sketches/Proof of Concept

Below is a **640x480 rectangle**, representing your game screen. Label the bottom-left corner as the coordinate (0,0). Then label the other four corners. Then, in the rectangle, sketch a picture of your game!

Order of Operations

If you were to write instructions for getting ready for school, it would matter very much which instruction came first: putting on your socks, putting on your shoes, etc.

Sometimes we need multiple expressions in mathematics, and the order matters there, too! Mathematicians didn't always agree on the **Order of Operations**, but at some point it became important to develop rules to help them work together.

To help us organize our math into something we can trust, we can *diagram* a math expression using the **Circles of Evaluation**. For example, the expression $(1 - 4) \div (10 \times 7)$ can be diagrammed as shown below.

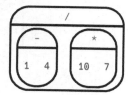

Order of Operations is important when programming, too!

To convert a **Circle of Evaluation** into Code, we walk through the circle from outside-in, moving left-to-right. We type an open parenthesis when we *start* a circle, and a close parenthesis when we *end* one. Once we're in a circle, we first write the **function** at the top, then write the inputs from left to right. The circle above, for example, would be programmed as `(/ (- 1 4) (* 10 7))`.

Completing Circles of Evaluation from Arithmetic Expressions

For each expression on the left, finish the Circle of Evaluation on the right by filling in the blanks.

	Arithmetic Expression	Circle of Evaluation
1	$4 + 2 - \dfrac{10}{5}$	
2	$7 - 1 + 5 \times 8$	
3	$\dfrac{-15}{5 + -8}$	
4	$(4 + (9 - 8)) \times 5$	
5	$6 \times 4 + \dfrac{9 - -6}{5}$	
★	$\dfrac{20}{6 + 4} - \dfrac{5 \times 9}{-12 - 3}$	

Matching Circles of Evaluation and Arithmetic Expressions

Draw a line from each Circle of Evaluation on the left to the corresponding arithmetic expression on the right.

Circle of Evaluation		Arithmetic Expression

1   A $1 \div (1 \times 1)$

2   B $(1 + 1) - 1$

3   C $(1 \times 1) \div 1$

4   D $(1 + (1 - 1)) \times (1 + 1)$

5   E $(1 - 1) \times (1 + 1)$

Translate Arithmetic to Circles of Evaluation & Code (Intro)

Translate each of the arithmetic expressions below into Circles of Evaluation, then translate them to Code.

	Arithmetic	Circle of Evaluation	Code
1	$(3 \times 7) - (1 + 2)$		
2	$3 - (1 + 2)$		
3	$3 - (1 + (5 \times 6))$		
4	$(1 + (5 \times 6)) - 3$		

Completing Partial Code from Circles of Evaluation

For each Circle of Evaluation on the left, finish the Code on the right by filling in the blanks.

	Circle of Evaluation	Code
1	+ / 16 / * / 6 -3	(+ _____ (* 6 _____))
2	− / + / 25 13 / * / 2 4	(_____ (+ _____ 13) (_____ _____ 4))
3	* / + / 10 4 / 28	(_____ (+ _____ 4) _____)
4	* / 13 / / / 7 / + / 2 −4	(_____ 13 (_____ 7 (_____ 2 −4)))
5	+ / / / + / 8 1 / 3 / − / 5 3	(_____ (_____ (_____ 8 1) 3) (_____ 5 3))
6	/ / + / 7 9 / * / 2 4	(/ (+ _____ _____) (* _____ _____))

Matching Circles of Evaluation & Code

Draw a line from each Circle of Evaluation on the left to the corresponding Code on the right.

Circle of Evaluation		Code

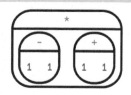

1   A   `( * ( - 1 ( + 1 1)) 1)`

2   B   `( * ( - 1 1) ( + 1 1))`

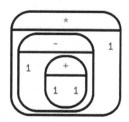

3   C   `( * ( + 1 1) ( - ( + 1 1) 1))`

4   D   `( - ( + 1 1) 1)`

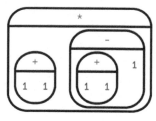

5   E   `( + ( - 1 1) 1)`

Translate each of the arithmetic expressions below into Circles of Evaluation, then translate them to Code.

	Arithmetic	Circle of Evaluation	Code
1	$6 \times 8 + (7 - 23)$		
2	$18 \div 2 + 24 \times 4 - 2$		
3	$(22 - 7) \div (3 + 2)$		
4	$(24 \div 4) \times 2 - 6 + 20 \times 2$		

Arithmetic Expressions to Circles of Evaluation & Code-Challenge

Translate each of the arithmetic expressions below into Circles of Evaluation, then translate them to Code. Hint: Two useful functions are `sqr` and `sqrt`.

	Arithmetic	Circle of Evaluation	Code
1	$\dfrac{16 + 3^2}{\sqrt{49} - 2}$		
2	$45 - 9 \times (3 + (2 - 4)) - 7$		
3	$(50 \div 5) \times 2 - ((3 + 4) \times 2 - 5)$		

Introduction to Programming

The **Editor** is a software program we use to write Code. Our Editor allows us to experiment with Code on the right-hand side, in the **Interactions Area**. For Code that we want to *keep*, we can put it on the left-hand side in the **Definitions Area**. Clicking the "Run" button causes the computer to re-read everything in the Definitions Area and erase anything that was typed into the Interactions Area.

Data Types

Programming languages involve different *data types*, such as Numbers, Strings, Booleans, and even Images.

- Numbers are values like `1`, `0.4`, `1/3`, and `-8261.003`.
    - Numbers are *usually* used for quantitative data and other values are *usually* used as categorical data.

- Strings are values like `"Emma"`, `"Rosanna"`, `"Jen and Ed"`, or even `"08/28/1980"`.
    - All strings *must* be surrounded in quotation marks.

- Booleans are either `true` or `false`.

All values evaluate to themselves. The program `42` will evaluate to `42`, the String `"Hello"` will evaluate to `"Hello"`, and the Boolean `false` will evaluate to `false`.

Operators

Operators (like `+`, `-`, `*`, `<`, etc.) are treated the same way as functions: after all, they have inputs and outputs and obey the same rules!

Applying Functions

Applying functions (and operators!) works much the way it does in math. Every function has a name, takes some inputs, and produces some output. The function name is written first, followed by a list of *arguments*.

- In math this could look like $f(5)$ or $g(10, 4)$.
- In WeScheme, these examples would be written as `(f 5)` and `(g 10 4)`.
- Appling the operator `+` to the inputs 1 and 2 would look like `( 1 2)`.
- Applying a function to make images would look like `(star 50 "solid" "red")`.
- There are many other functions, for example `num-sqr`, `num-sqrt`, `triangle`, `square`, `string-repeat`, etc.

Functions have *contracts*, which help explain how a function should be used. Every contract has three parts:

- The *Name* of the function - literally, what it's called.
- The *Domain* of the function - what *types of values* the function consumes, and in what order.
- The *Range* of the function - what *type of value* the function produces.

Numbers and Strings

Make sure you've loaded the wescheme.org editor, clicked "Run", and are working in the *Interactions Area*.

Numbers

1) Try typing `42` into the Interactions Area and hitting "Enter". What is the largest number the editor can handle?

_____

2) Try typing `0.5`. Then try typing `.5`. Then try clicking on the answer. Experiment with other decimals. Explain what you understand about how decimals work in this programming language. _____

_____

_____

_____

3) What happens if you try a fraction like `1/3`? _____

_____

4) Try writing **negative** integers, fractions and decimals. What do you learn? _____

Wescheme can handle negatives. _____

Strings

String values are always in quotes.

5) Is `42` the same as `"42"`? Why or why not? Write your answer below:

_____

- Try typing your name *(in quotes!)*.
- Try typing a sentence like `"I'm excited to learn to code!"` *(in quotes!)*.
- Try typing your name with the opening quote, but *without the closing quote.* Read the error message!
- Now try typing your name *without any quotes.* Read the error message!

6) Explain what you understand about how strings work in this programming language. _____

_____

_____

Booleans

Boolean-producing expressions are yes-or-no questions and will always evaluate to either `true` ("yes") or `false` ("no"). What will each of the expressions below evaluate to? *Write down your prediction in the blanks provided and then type the code into the Interactions Area to see what it returns.*

	Prediction	Result		Prediction	Result
1) `(<= 3 4)`	_____	_____	2) `(string>? "a" "b")`	_____	_____
3) `(= 3 2)`	_____	_____	4) `(string<? "a" "b")`	_____	_____
5) `(< 2 4)`	_____	_____	6) `(string=? "a" "b")`	_____	_____
7) `(>= 5 5)`	_____	_____	8) `(string<>? "a" "a")`	_____	_____
9) `(>= 4 6)`	_____	_____	10) `(string>=? "a" "a")`	_____	_____
11) `(<> 3 3)`	_____	_____	12) `(string<>? "a" "b")`	_____	_____

13) In your own words, describe what `<` does.

_____

14) In your own words, describe what `>=` does.

_____

15) In your own words, describe what `<>` does.

_____

	Prediction:	Result:
16) `(string=? "a tree" "trees")`	_____	_____
17) `(string=? "tree" "tree")`	_____	_____
18) `(string-contains? "catnap" "cat")`	_____	_____
19) `(string-contains? "cat" "catnap")`	_____	_____

20) How many **Numbers** are there in the entire universe? _____

21) How many **Strings** are there in the entire universe? _____

22) How many **Booleans** are there in the entire universe? _____

Applying Functions

Type this line of code into the Interactions Area and hit "Enter":

```
(triangle 50 "solid" "red")
```

1) What is the name of this function? _____

2) What did the expression evaluate to? _____

3) How many arguments does `triangle` expect? _____

4) What data type does the `triangle` function produce? _____

Catching Bugs

5) `(triangle 20 "solid")`

> **<u>triangle</u>**: expects 3 arguments, but given 2: <u>20</u> <u>solid</u> at: line 1, column 0, in <interactions>

Can you spot the mistake? _____

6) `(triangle "solid" "red" 20)`

> **<u>triangle</u>**: expects a non-negative number as 1st argument, but given: <u>solid</u>; other arguments were: <u>red</u> <u>20</u> at: line 1, column 0, in <interactions>

Can you spot the mistake? _____

7) `(triangle 20 40 "solid" "red")`

> **<u>triangle</u>**: expects 3 arguments, but given 4: <u>20</u> <u>40</u> <u>solid</u> <u>red</u> at: line 1, column 0, in <interactions>

Can you spot the mistake? _____

8) `(triangle 20 solid "red")`

> **<u>solid</u>**: this variable is not defined at: line 1, column 0, in <interactions>

Can you spot the mistake? _____

9) `(triangle 20 "striped" "red")`

> **<u>triangle</u>**: expects a style ("solid" / "outline") or an opacity value [0-255]) as 2nd argument, but given: <u>"striped"</u>; other arguments were: <u>20</u> <u>"red"</u> at: line 1, column 0, in <interactions>

Can you spot the mistake? _____

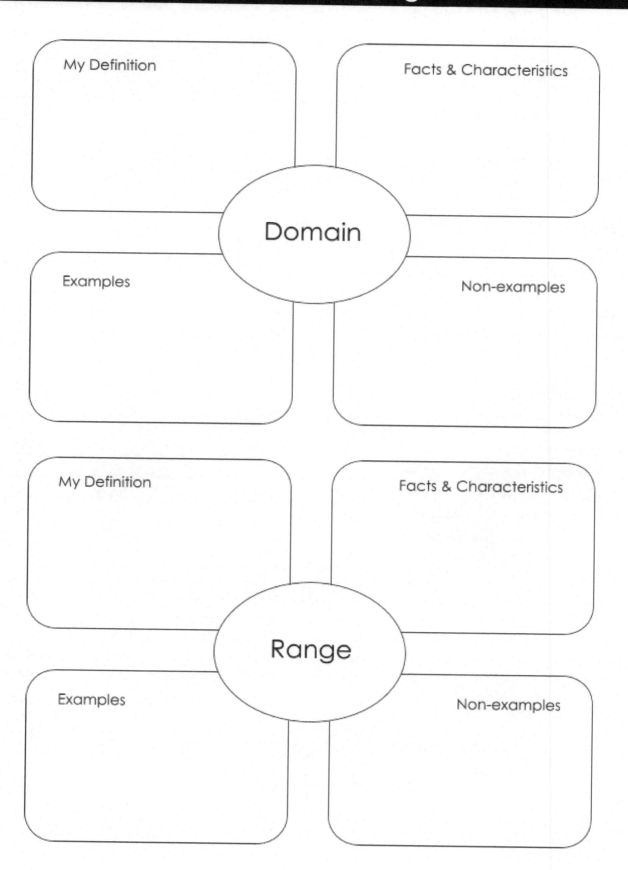

My Definition

Facts & Characteristics

Domain

Examples

Non-examples

My Definition

Facts & Characteristics

Range

Examples

Non-examples

Practicing Contracts: Domain & Range

Consider the following contract:

```
is-beach-weather :: Number, String -> Boolean
```

1) What is the **Name** of this function? _____

2) How many arguments are in this function's **Domain**? _____

3) What is the **Type** of this function's **first argument**? _____

4) What is the **Type** of this function's **second argument**? _____

5) What is the **Range** of this function? _____

6) Circle the expression below that shows the correct application of this function, based on its contract.

A. `(is-beach-weather 70 90)`

B. `(is-beach-weather 80 100 "cloudy")`

C. `(is-beach-weather "sunny" 90)`

D. `(is-beach-weather 90 "stormy weather")`

Consider the following contract:

```
cylinder :: Number, Number, String -> Image
```

7) What is the **Name** of this function? _____

8) How may arguments are in this function's **Domain**? _____

9) What is the **Type** of this function's **first argument**? _____

10) What is the **Type** of this function's **second argument**? _____

11) What is the **Type** of this function's **third argument**? _____

12) What is the **Range** of this function? _____

13) Circle the expression below that shows the correct application of this function, based on its contract.

A. `(cylinder "red" 10 60)`

B. `(cylinder 30 "green")`

C. `(cylinder 10 25 "blue")`

D. `(cylinder 14 "orange" 25)`

Matching Expressions and Contracts

Match the contract (left) with the expression described by the function being used (right).

	Contract			Expression
	; make-id :: String, Number -> Image	1	A	(make-id "Savannah" "Lopez" 32)
	; make-id :: String, Number, String -> Image	2	B	(make-id "Pilar" 17)
	; make-id :: String -> Image	3	C	(make-id "Akemi" 39 "red")
	; make-id :: String, String -> Image	4	D	(make-id "Raïssa" "McCracken")
	; make-id :: String, String, Number -> Image	5	E	(make-id "von Einsiedel")

	Contract			Expression
	; is-capital :: String, String -> Boolean	6	A	(show-pop "Juneau" "AK" 31848)
	; is-capital :: String, String, String -> Boolean	7	B	(show-pop "San Juan" 395426)
	; show-pop :: String, Number -> Image	8	C	(is-capital "Accra" "Ghana")
	; show-pop :: String, String, Number -> Image	9	D	(show-pop 3751351 "Oklahoma")
	; show-pop :: Number, String -> Number	10	E	(is-capital "Albany" "NY" "USA")

Using Contracts

`ellipse:: Number, Number, String, String -> Image`

	Use the contract to write an expression that generates a similar image:
	Use the contract to write an expression that generates a similar image:
What changes with the first Number?	
What about the shape changes with the second Number?	
Write an expression using `ellipse` to produce a circle.	

`regular-polygon:: Number, Number, String, String -> Image`

	Use the contract to write an expression that generates a similar image:
	Use the contract to write an expression that generates a similar image:
What changes with the first Number?	
What about the shape changes with the second Number?	
Use `regular-polygon` to write an expression for a square!	
How would you describe a **regular polygon** to a friend?	

1) What kind of triangle does the `triangle` function produce? _____

There are lots of other kinds of triangles! And WeScheme has lots of other functions that make triangles!

```
triangle :: (size:: Number, style :: String, color :: String) -> Image
right-triangle :: (base::Number, height::Number, style::String, color::String) -> Image
isosceles-triangle :: (leg::Number, angle::Number, style::String, color::String) -> Image
```

2) Why do you think `triangle` only needs one number, while `right-triangle` and `isosceles-triangle` need two numbers and `triangle/sas` needs three?

_____

_____

3) Write `right-triangle` expressions for the images below. *One argument for each should be* `100` .

_____

_____

4) What do you think the numbers in `right-triangle` represent? _____

5) Write `isosceles-triangle` expressions for the images below. *1 argument for each should be* `100` .

_____

_____

6) What do you think the numbers in `isosceles-triangle` represent?

_____

7) Write 2 expressions that would build **right-isosceles** triangles. Use `right-triangle` for one expression and `isosceles-triangle` for the other expression.

_____

_____

Radial Star

```
radial-star :: (
    points :: Number,
    inner-radius :: Number,
    full-radius :: Number,
    style :: String,
    color :: String
) -> Image
```

Using the detailed contract above, match each image to the expression that describes it.

Image			Expression
	1	A	(radial-star 5 50 200 "solid" "black")
	2	B	(radial-star 7 100 200 "solid" "black")
	3	C	(radial-star 7 100 200 "outline" "black")
	4	D	(radial-star 10 150 200 "solid" "black")
	5	E	(radial-star 10 20 200 "solid" "black")
	6	F	(radial-star 100 20 200 "outline" "black")
	7	G	(radial-star 100 100 200 "outline" "black")

What's on your mind?

Diagramming Function Composition

f :: Number -> Number Consumes a number, multiplies by 3 to produce the result	g :: Number -> Number Consumes a number, adds six to produce the result	h :: Number -> Number Consumes a number, subtracts one to produce the result
$f(x) = 3x$	$g(x) = x + 6$	$h(x) = x - 1$

For each function composition diagrammed below, translate it into the equivalent Circle of Evaluation for Order of Operations. Then write expressions for *both* versions of the Circles of Evaluation, and evaluate them for $x = 4$. The first one has been completed for you.

Function Composition	Order of Operations	Translate & Evaluate	
1)		Composition:	`(h (g (f x)))`
		Operations:	`(- (+ (* 3 x) 6) 1)`
		Evaluate for x = 4	$h(g(f(4))) = 17$
2)		Composition:	
		Operations:	
		Evaluate for x = 4	
3)		Composition:	
		Operations:	
		Evaluate for x = 4	
4)		Composition:	
		Operations:	
		Evaluate for x = 4	

1) Draw a Circle of Evaluation and write the Code for a **solid, green star, size 50**.

Circle of Evaluation:

Code: _____

Using the star described above as the **original**, draw the Circles of Evaluation and write the Code for each exercise below.

2) A solid, green star, that is triple the size of the original (using `scale`)	3) A solid, green star, that is half the size of the original (using `scale`)
4) A solid, green star of size 50 that has been rotated 45 degrees counter-clockwise	5) A solid, green star that is 3 times the size of the original **and** has been rotated 45 degrees

Function Composition — Your Name

You'll be investigating these functions with your partner:

```
; text :: String, Number, String -> Image        ; frame :: Image -> Image
; flip-horizontal :: Image -> Image              ; above :: Image, Image -> Image
; flip-vertical :: Image -> Image                ; beside :: Image, Image -> Image
```

1) In the editor, write the code to make an image of your name in big letters in a color of your choosing using `text`. Then draw the Circle of Evaluation and write the Code that will create the image.

Circle of Evaluation:

Code: _____

Using the "image of your name" described above as the **original**, draw the Circles of Evaluation and write the Code for each exercise below. Test your ideas in the editor to make sure they work.

2) The framed "image of your name".	3) The "image of your name" flipped vertically.
4) The "image of your name" above "the image of your name" flipped vertically.	5) The "image of your name" flipped horizontally beside "the image of your name".

Function Composition — scale-xy

You'll be investigating these two functions with your partner:

```
; scale/xy :: Number, Number, Image -> Image          ; overlay :: Image, Image -> Image
```

The Image:	Circle of Evaluation:	Code:
	rhombus 40 90 "solid" "purple"	`(rhombus 40 90 "solid" "purple")`

Starting with the image described above, write the Circles of Evaluation and Code for each exercise below. Be sure to test your code in the editor!

1) A purple rhombus that is stretched 4 times as wide.	2) A purple rhombus that is stretched 4 times as tall

3) The tall rhombus from #1 overlayed on the wide rhombus (#2).	★ Overlay a red rhombus onto the last image you made in #3.

More than one way to Compose an Image!

What image will each of the four expressions below evaluate to? If you're not sure, type them into the Interactions Area and see if you can figure out how the code constructs its image.

```
(beside (rectangle 200 100 "solid" "black")(square 100 "solid" "black"))

(scale/xy 1 2(square 100 "solid" "black"))

(scale 2 (rectangle 100 100 "solid" "black"))

(above
   (rectangle 100 50 "solid" "black")
   (above
      (rectangle 200 100 "solid" "black")
      (rectangle 100 50 "solid" "black")))
```

For each image below, identify 2 expressions that could be used to compose it. The bank of expressions at the top of the page includes one possible option for each image.

1

2

3

★

Defining Values

In math, we use **values** like -98.1, $2/3$ and 42. In math, we also use **expressions** like 1×3, $\sqrt{16}$, and $5 - 2$. These evaluate to results, and typing any of them in as code produces some answer.

Math also has **definitions**. These are different from values and expressions, because *they do not produce results*. Instead, they simply create names for values, so that those names can be re-used to make the Math simpler and more efficient.

Definitions always have both a name and an expression. The name goes on the left and the value-producing expression goes on the right, separated by an equals sign:

$x = 4$

$y = 9 + x$

The name is defined to be the result of evaluating the expression. Using the above examples, we get "x is defined to be 4, and y is defined to be 13". **Important: there is no "answer" to a definition**, and typing in a definition as code will produce no result.

Notice that *definitions can refer to previous definitions*. In the example above, the definition of y refers to x. But x, on the other hand, *cannot* refer to y. Once a value has been defined, it can be used in later expressions.

In WeScheme, these definitions are written a little differently, making it clear that we're talking about definitions:
Try typing these definitions into the Definitions Area on the left, clicking "Run", and then *using* them in the Interactions Area on the right.

```
(define x 4)
(define y (+ 9 x))
```

Just like in math, definitions in our programming language can only refer to previously-defined values.

Here are a few more value definitions. Feel free to type them in, and make sure you understand them.

```
(define x (+ 5 1))
(define y (* x 7))
(define food "Pizza!")
(define dot (circle y "solid" "red"))
```

Open the Defining Values Starter File and click "Run".

1) What do you Notice?

_____

_____

_____

2) What do you Wonder?

_____

_____

_____

Look at the expressions listed below. Think about what you expect each of them to produce. Then, test them out one at a time in the Interactions Area.

- x
- (+ x 5)
- (- y 9)
- (* x y)
- z
- t
- gold-star
- my-name
- swamp
- 5pi

3) What have you learned about defining values?

_____

_____

_____

_____

4) Define at least 2 more variables in the Definitions Area, click "Run" and test them out. Once you know they're working, record the code you used below.

_____

_____

_____

_____

1) What image do you see repeated in the flag? _____

2) In the code below, highlight or circle all instances of the expression that makes the repeated image.

```
(define China
  (put-image (
    rotate 40 (star 15 "solid" "yellow"))
    120 175
      (put-image (
        rotate 80 (star 15 "solid" "yellow"))
        140 150
          (put-image (
            rotate 60 (star 15 "solid" "yellow"))
            140 120
              (put-image (
                rotate 40 (star 15 "solid" "yellow"))
                120 90
                  (put-image (
                    scale 3 (star 15 "solid" "yellow"))
                    60 140
                      (rectangle 300 200 "solid" "red")))))))
```

3) Write the code to define a value for the repeated expression.

_____

4) Open the <u>Chinese Flag Starter File</u> and click "Run".

- Type `china` into the Interactions Area and click **Enter**.

- **Save a copy** of the file, and simplify the flag code using the value you defined.

- Click "Run", and confirm that you still get the same image as the original.

- Now change the color of all of the stars to black, in both files.

- Then change the size of the stars.

5) Why is it helpful to define values for repeated images?

_____

_____

Challenge:

- This file uses a function we haven't seen before! What is it? _____

- Can you figure out its contract? *Hint: Focus on the last instance of the function.*

_____

1) Complete the table using the first row as an example.

2) Write the code to define the value of sunny. _____

Original Circle of Evaluation & Code	→	Use the *defined value* sunny to simplify!

scale
3
radial-star
30 20 50 "solid" "yellow"

→

scale
3
sunny

Code:
(scale 3 (radial-star 30 20 50 "solid" "yellow"))

→

Code:
(scale 3 sunny)

frame
radial-star
30 20 50 "solid" "yellow"

→

Code:
(frame (radial-star 30 20 50 "solid" "yellow"))

→

Code:

overlay
text
"sun" 30 "black"
radial-star
30 20 50 "solid" "yellow"

→

→

Code:
(overlay (text "sun" 30 "black") (radial-star 30 20 50 "solid" "yellow"))

→

Code:

3) Test your code in the editor and make sure it produces what you would expect it to.

Which Value(s) Would it Make Sense to Define?

For each of the images below, identify which element(s) you would want to define before writing code to compose the image.

Hint: what gets repeated?

Writing Code using Defined Values

1) On the line below, **write the Code** to define PRIZE-STAR as a pink, outline star of size 65.

_____

Using the PRIZE-STAR definition from above, draw the Circle of Evaluation and write the Code for each of the exercises. One Circle of Evaluation has been done for you.

---

2) The outline of a pink star that is three times the size of the original (using scale)

Circle of Evaluation:

```
        scale
   3   PRIZE-STAR
```

Code:

---

3) The outline of a pink star that is half the size of the original (using scale)

Circle of Evaluation:

Code:

---

4) The outline of a pink star that is rotated 45 degrees

(It should be the same size as the original.)

Circle of Evaluation:

Code:

---

5) The outline of a pink star that is three times as big as the original **and** has been rotated 45 degrees

Circle of Evaluation:

Code:

---

6) How does defining values help you as a programmer?

_____

_____

_____

Estimating Coordinates

```
(define dot (circle 50 "solid" "red"))
(define background (rectangle 300 200 "outline" "black"))
```

Think of the background image as a sheet of graph paper with the origin (0,0) in the bottom left corner. The width of the rectangle is 300 and the height is 200. The numbers in `put-image` specify a point on that graph paper, where the center of the top image (in this case `dot`) should be placed.

Estimate: What coordinates for the `dot` created each of the following images?

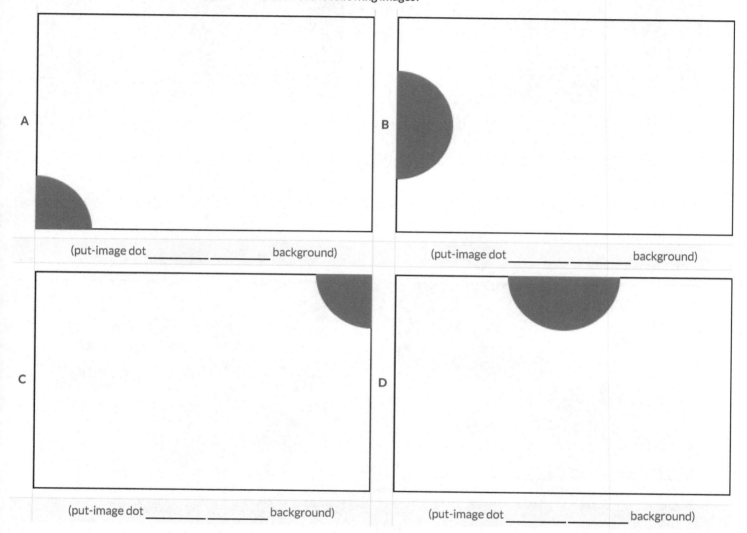

A

(put-image dot _____ _____ background)

B

(put-image dot _____ _____ background)

C

(put-image dot _____ _____ background)

D

(put-image dot _____ _____ background)

Decomposing Flags

Each of the flags below is shown with their width and height. Identify the shapes that make up each flag. Use the flag's dimensions to estimate the dimensions of the different shapes. Then estimate the x and y coordinates for the point at which the center of each shape should be located on the flag. *Hint: The bottom left corner of each flag is at (0,0) and the top right corner is given by the flags dimensions.*

Cameroon (450 x 300)

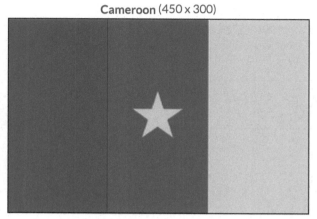

shape:	color:	width:	height:	x	y

Chile (420 x 280)

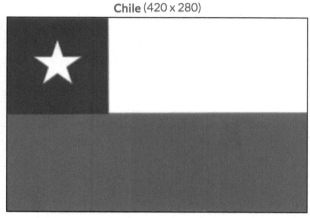

shape:	color:	width:	height:	x	y

Panama (300 x 200)

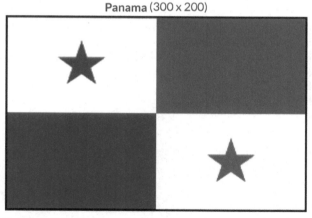

shape:	color:	width:	height:	x	y

Norway (330 x 240)

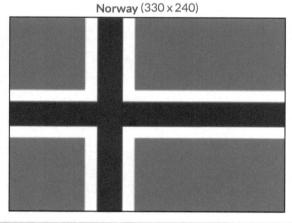

shape:	color:	width:	height:	x	y

Notice and Wonder

As you investigate the Blank Game Starter File with your partner, record what you Notice, and then what you Wonder.

Remember, "Notices" are statements, not questions.

What do you Notice?	What do you Wonder?

The Great gt domain debate!

Kermit: The domain of `gt` is `Number, String, String`.

Oscar: The domain of `gt` is `Number`.

Ernie: I'm not sure who's right!

In order to make a triangle, we need a size, a color and a fill style...

but all we had to tell our actor was (`gt 20`) ...and they returned (`triangle 20 "solid" "green"`).

Please help us!

1) What is the correct domain for gt?

_____

2) What could you tell Ernie to help him understand how you know?

_____

_____

_____

_____

_____

_____

_____

_____

_____

Let's Define Some New Functions!

1) **Let's define a function** `rs` **to generate solid red squares of whatever size we give them!**

If I say (`rs 5`) , what would our actor need to say?

_____

Let's write a few more examples:

(rs _____) → _____

(rs _____) → _____

(rs _____) → _____

What changes in these examples? Name your variable(s): _____

Let's define our function using the variable.

(define (rs _____) _____)

2) **Let's define a function** `bigc` **to generate big solid circles of size 100 in whatever color we give them!**

If I say (`bigc "orange"`) , what would our actor need to say?

_____

Let's write a few more examples:

(bigc _____) → _____

(bigc _____) → _____

(bigc _____) → _____

What changes in these examples? Name your variable(s): _____

Let's define our function using the variable.

(define (bigc _____) _____)

3) **Let's define a function** `ps` **to build a pink star of size 50, with the input determining whether it's solid or outline!**

If I say (`ps "outline"`) , what would our actor need to say?

_____

Write examples for all other possible inputs:

(ps _____) → _____

(ps _____) → _____

What changes in these examples? Name your variable(s): _____

Let's define our function using the variable.

(define (ps _____) _____)

Add these new function definitions to your gt Starter File and test them out!

Let's Define Some More New Functions!

1) Let's define a function `sun` **to write SUNSHINE in whatever color and size we give it!**

If I say (`sun 5 "blue"`) , what would our actor need to say?

_____

Let's write a few more examples:

(sun _____ _____) → _____

(sun _____ _____) → _____

(sun _____ _____) → _____

What changes in these examples? Name your variable(s): _____

Let's define our function using the variable.

(define (sun _____ _____) _____)

2) Let's define a function `me` **to generate your name in whatever size and color we give it!**

If I say (`me 18 "gold"`) , what would our actor need to say?

_____

Let's write a few more examples:

(me _____ _____) → _____

(me _____ _____) → _____

(me _____ _____) → _____

What changes in these examples? Name your variable(s): _____

Let's define our function using the variable.

(define (me _____ _____) _____)

3) Let's define a function `gr` **to build a solid, green rectangle of whatever length and width we give it!**

If I say (`gr 10 80`) , what would our actor need to say?

_____

Let's write a few more examples:

(gr _____ _____) → (rectangle _____ _____ "solid" "green")

(gr _____ _____) → (rectangle _____ _____ "solid" "green")

(gr _____ _____) → (rectangle _____ _____ "solid" "green")

What changes in these examples? Name your variable(s): _____

Let's define our function using the variable.

(define (gr _____ _____) _____)

4) _Add these new function definitions to your_ <u>gt Starter File</u> _and test them out!_

Describe and Define Your Own Functions!

1) Let's define a function _____ **to generate...**

_____

If I say _____, what would our actor need to say? _____

Let's write a few more examples:

`((?FITB 5em) (?FITB 10em)) → ((?FITB 6em) (?FITB 25em))`

`((?FITB 5em) (?FITB 10em)) → ((?FITB 6em) (?FITB 25em))`

`((?FITB 5em) (?FITB 10em)) → ((?FITB 6em) (?FITB 25em))`

What variable changes? _____

Let's define our function using the variable.

`fun` _____ (_____) : _____ (_____) `end`

2) Let's define a function _____ **to generate...**

_____

If I say _____, what would our actor need to say? _____

Let's write a few more examples:

`((?FITB 5em) (?FITB 10em)) → ((?FITB 6em) (?FITB 25em))`

`((?FITB 5em) (?FITB 10em)) → ((?FITB 6em) (?FITB 25em))`

`((?FITB 5em) (?FITB 10em)) → ((?FITB 6em) (?FITB 25em))`

What variable changes? _____

Let's define our function using the variable.

`fun` _____ (_____) : _____ (_____) `end`

3) Let's define a function _____ **to generate...**

_____

If I say _____, what would our actor need to say? _____

Let's write a few more examples:

`((?FITB 5em) (?FITB 10em)) → ((?FITB 6em) (?FITB 25em))`

`((?FITB 5em) (?FITB 10em)) → ((?FITB 6em) (?FITB 25em))`

`((?FITB 5em) (?FITB 10em)) → ((?FITB 6em) (?FITB 25em))`

What variable changes? _____

Let's define our function using the variable.

`fun` _____ (_____) : _____ (_____) `end`

Add your new function definitions to your gt Starter File and test them out!

What's on your mind?

Identifying Functions from Graphs

Decide whether each graph below is a function. If it's not, prove it by drawing a vertical line that crosses the plot at more than one point.

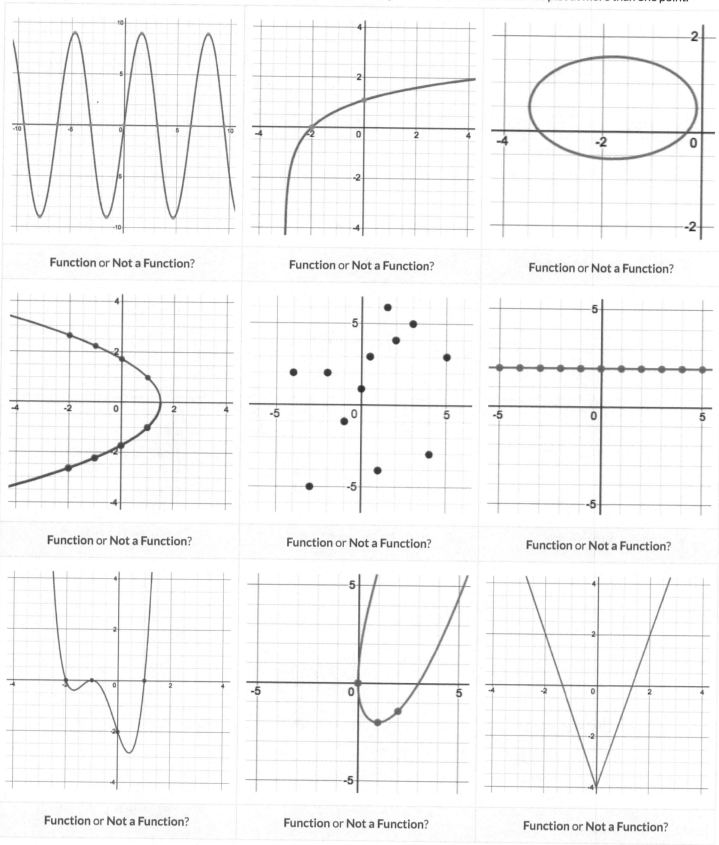

Function or **Not a Function**?

Function or **Not a Function**?

Function or **Not a Function**?

Function or **Not a Function**?

Function or **Not a Function**?

Function or **Not a Function**?

Function or **Not a Function**?

Function or **Not a Function**?

Function or **Not a Function**?

Decide whether each graph below is a function. If it's not, prove it by drawing a vertical line that crosses the plot at more than one point.

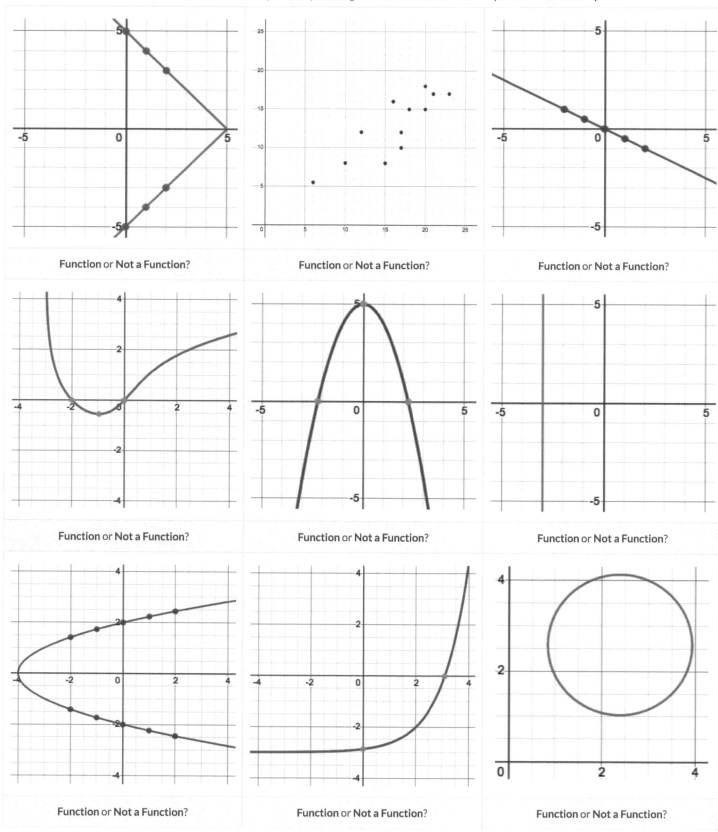

Function or **Not a Function?**

Function or **Not a Function?**

Function or **Not a Function?**

Function or **Not a Function?**

Function or **Not a Function?**

Function or **Not a Function?**

Function or **Not a Function?**

Function or **Not a Function?**

Function or **Not a Function?**

Notice and Wonder - Functions

Write down what you Notice and Wonder about the graphs you've just seen. (At a future point you will also use this page to record what you notice and wonder about the tables you'll see). *Remember: "Notices" should be statements, not questions.*

What do you Notice?	What do you Wonder?

How Tables Fail the Vertical Line Test

1) Each of the graphs below is also represented by a table. Use the vertical line test to determine whether or not each graph represents a function.

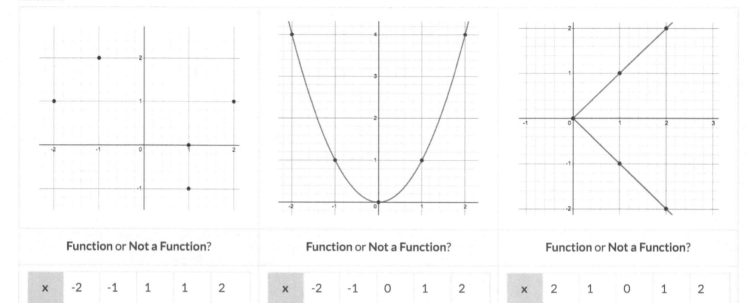

	Function or Not a Function?						Function or Not a Function?						Function or Not a Function?				

x	-2	-1	1	1	2
y	1	2	0	-1	1

x	-2	-1	0	1	2
y	4	1	0	1	4

x	2	1	0	1	2
y	2	-1	0	-1	-2

2) For each graph that failed the vertical line test, label the offending points with their coordinates.

3) Find the same coordinates in the table below the graph and circle or highlight them.

4) What do the tables of the non-functions have in common? What could you look for in other tables to identify whether or not they could represent a function?

_____

_____

_____

5) Use the process you just described to determine whether each table below could represent a function. Circle or highlight the points that would end up on the same vertical line.

x	y
0	-2
1	-2
2	-2
3	-2
4	-2

x	y
0	-2
1	1
2	4
3	7
3	10

x	y
0	3
1	4
-1	5
2	6
-2	7

x	y
1	0
0	1
1	2
2	3
3	4

Function or Not?   **Function or Not?**   **Function or Not?**   **Function or Not?**

Identifying Functions from Tables

Decide whether or not each table below could represent a function. If not, circle what you see that tells you it's not a function. *In a function, there is exactly one y-value (or output) for each x-value (or input). If a table has more than one y-value (or output) for the same x-value (or input), it can not represent a function.*

x	y
0	3
1	2
2	5
3	6
4	5

Function or **Not?**

x	y
5	3
1	4
-3	5
3	6
2	7

Function or **Not?**

input	output
0	2
5	2
2	2
6	2
3	2

Function or **Not?**

x	y
1	0
1	1
1	2
1	3
1	4

Function or **Not?**

tickets	$
2	0
1	2
2	4
3	6
4	8

Function or **Not?**

input	output
-4	-2
-3	-1
-2	0
-1	1
0	2

Function or **Not?**

x	y
10	9
3	2
9	8
17	16
3	5

Function or **Not?**

C	F
-40	-40
0	32
10	50
37	98.6
100	212

Function or **Not?**

input	output
0	7
-1	2
4	3
8	6
-5	-8

Function or **Not?**

$	games
10	5
11	25
12	45
13	65
14	85

Function or **Not?**

x	y
8	10
6	5
4	0
6	-5
8	-10

Function or **Not?**

miles	minutes
0	0
1	2
2	4
3	6
4	8

Function or **Not?**

Identifying Functions from Tables & Graphs

Decide whether or not each table or graph below could represent a function. If not, circle what tells you it's not a function. *In a function, there is exactly one y-value for each x-value. If a table has more than one y-value for the same x-value, it can not represent a function.*

x	y
−2	5
0	2
2	4
4	7
6	8

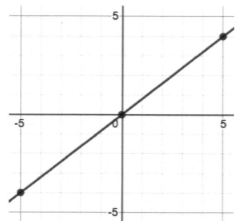

x	y
0	7
1	2
1	3
2	6
3	−8

Function or Not a Function?   **Function or Not a Function?**   **Function or Not a Function?**

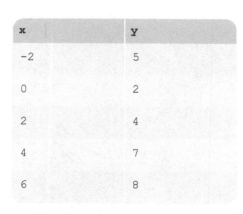

x	y
−1.5	−2
−1	−1
−0.5	0
0	1
0.5	2

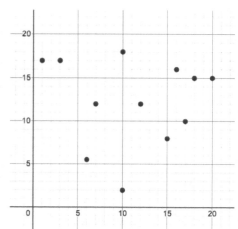

Function or Not a Function?   **Function or Not a Function?**   **Function or Not a Function?**

x	y
−1	1.5
0	1.5
1	1.5
2	1.5
3	1.5

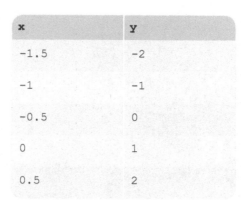

x	y
8	1
5	2
4	3
5	4
8	5

Function or Not a Function?   **Function or Not a Function?**   **Function or Not a Function?**

Matching Examples and Definitions (Math)

Match each of the function definitions on the left with the corresponding table on the right.

It may help to circle or highlight what's changing in the $f(x)$ column of the table!

Function Definitions

$f(x) = x - 2$ 1

$f(x) = 2x$ 2

$f(x) = 2x + 1$ 3

$f(x) = 1 - 2x$ 4

$f(x) = 2 + x$ 5

Example Tables

A

x	$f(x)$
1	2×1
2	2×2
3	2×3

B

x	$f(x)$
15	$15 - 2$
25	$25 - 2$
35	$35 - 2$

C

x	$f(x)$
10	$2 + 10$
15	$2 + 15$
20	$2 + 20$

D

x	$f(x)$
0	$1 - 2(0)$
1	$1 - 2(1)$
2	$1 - 2(2)$

E

x	$f(x)$
10	$2(10) + 1$
20	$2(20) + 1$
30	$2(30) + 1$

Function Notation - Substitution

Complete the table below, by substituting the given value into the expression and evaluating.

Function Definition	Expression	Substitution	Evaluates to
$f(x) = x + 2$	$f(3)$	$3 + 2$	5
$g(x) = x - 1$	$g(6)$		
$h(x) = 3x$	$h(4)$		
$k(x) = 2x - 1$	$k(5)$		

Now that you understand how to evaluate an expression, let's get some more practice! The table below includes four different functions. Beneath each of them are a collection of different expressions to evaluate.

$m(x) = -2x + 3$	$n(x) = -x + 7$	$v(x) = 10x - 8$	$w(x) = x^2$
$m(3) = -2(3) + 3$	$n(5) =$	$v(7) =$	$w(-2) =$
-3			
$m(-4) =$	$n(-2) =$	$v(0) =$	$w(10) =$
$m(0) =$	$n(3.5) =$	$v(-10) =$	$w(0) =$
$m(0.5) =$	$n(0) =$	$v(2.5) =$	$w(1.5) =$

What do you Notice?	What do you Wonder?

Function Notation - Graphs

Find the values described by the expressions below each graph.

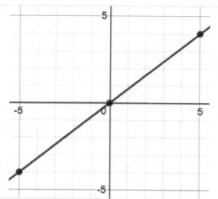

$f(-5) =$ _____

$f(5) =$ _____

$g(-2) =$ _____

$g(0) =$ _____

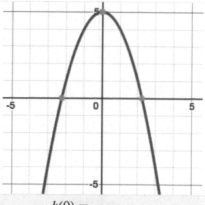

$h(0) =$ _____

$h(1) =$ _____

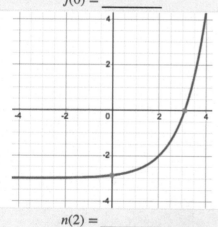

$j(-2) =$ _____

$j(0) =$ _____

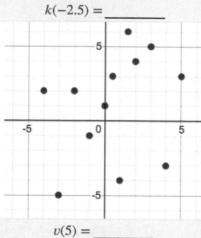

$k(3) =$ _____

$k(-2.5) =$ _____

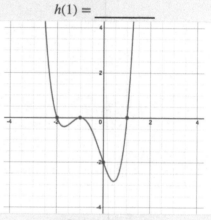

$m(0) =$ _____

$m(1) =$ _____

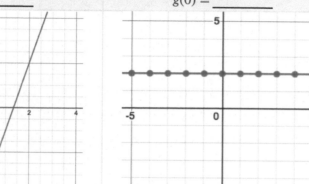

$n(2) =$ _____

$n(-\infty) =$ _____

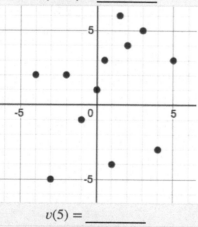

$v(5) =$ _____

$v(2) =$ _____

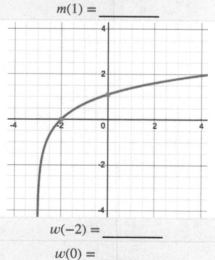

$w(-2) =$ _____

$w(0) =$ _____

Function Notation - Tables

Find the values described by the expressions below each table.

Note: not all of the relationships here are actually functions!

x	f(x)
0	0
1	2
2	4
3	6
4	8

$f(3) =$ _____

$f(4) =$ _____

x	g(x)
5	3
1	4
-3	5
3	6
2	7

$g(1) =$ _____

$g(3) =$ _____

x	h(x)
0	2
5	2
2	2
6	2
3	2

$h(0) =$ _____

$h(3) =$ _____

x	y(x)
1	0
1	1
1	2
1	3
1	4

$y(1) =$ 0? 1? 2? 3? 4?

$y(8) =$ _____

a	b(a)
-4	-2
-3	-1
-2	0
-1	1
0	2

$b(-1) =$ _____

$b(0) =$ _____

c	d(c)
0	3
1	2
2	5
3	6
4	5

$d(2) =$ _____

$d(4) =$ _____

n	m(n)
0	0
-1	-1
-2	-2
-3	-3
-4	-4

$m(0) =$ _____

$m(-3) =$ _____

q	p(q)
2	0
1	2
2	4
3	6
4	8

$p(1) =$ _____

$p(2) =$ _____

s	r(s)
0	7
-1	2
4	3
8	6
-5	-8

$r(-1) =$ _____

$r(8) =$ _____

w	v(w)
10	5
11	25
12	45
13	65
14	85

$v(11) =$ _____

$v(14) =$ _____

y	z(y)
8	10
6	5
4	0
5	-5
8	-10

$z(6) =$ _____

$z(2) =$ _____

time	l(time)
10	9
3	2
9	8
17	16
5	5

$l(10) =$ _____

$l(3) =$ _____

Defining Functions

Functions can be viewed in *multiple representations*. You already know one of them: *Contracts*, which specify the Name, Domain, and Range of a function. Contracts are a way of thinking of functions as a *mapping* between one set of data and another. For example, a mapping from Numbers to Strings:

```
f :: Number -> String
```

Another way to view functions is with *Examples*. Examples are essentially input-output tables, showing what the function would do for a specific input:

In our programming language, we focus on the last two columns and write them as code:

```
(EXAMPLE (f 1) (+ 1 2))
(EXAMPLE (f 2) (+ 2 2))
(EXAMPLE (f 3) (+ 3 2))
(EXAMPLE (f 4) (+ 4 2))
```

Finally, we write a formal **function definition** ourselves. The pattern in the Examples becomes *abstract* (or "general"), replacing the inputs with *variables*. In the example below, the same definition is written in both math and code:

$$f(x) = x + 2$$

```
(define (f x) (+ x 2))
```

Look for connections between these three representations!

- The function name is always the same, whether looking at the Contract, Examples, or Definition.
- The number of inputs in the Examples is always the same as the number of types in the Domain, which is always the same as the number of variables in the Definition.
- The "what the function does" pattern in the Examples is almost the same in the Definition, but with specific inputs replaced by variables.

Matching Examples and Contracts

Match each set of examples (left) with the contract that best describes it (right).

Examples		Contract
(EXAMPLE (f 5) (/ 5 2)) (EXAMPLE (f 9) (/ 9 2)) (EXAMPLE (f 24) (/ 24 2))	1	A ; f :: Number -> Number
(EXAMPLE (f 1) (rectangle 1 1 "outline" "red")) (EXAMPLE (f 6) (rectangle 6 6 "outline" "red"))	2	B ; f :: String -> Image
(EXAMPLE (f "pink" 5) (star 5 "solid" "pink")) (EXAMPLE (f "blue" 8) (star 8 "solid" "blue"))	3	C ; f :: Number -> Image
(EXAMPLE (f "Hi!") (text "Hi!" 50 "red")) (EXAMPLE (f "Ciao!") (text "Ciao!" 50 "red"))	4	D ; f :: Number, String -> Image
(EXAMPLE (f 5 "outline") (star 5 "outline" "yellow")) (EXAMPLE (f 5 "solid") (star 5 "solid" "yellow"))	5	E ; f :: String, Number -> Image

59

Matching Examples and Function Definitions

Highlight the variables in `gt` and label them with the word "size".

`(EXAMPLE (gt 20) (triangle 20 "solid" "green"))`

`(EXAMPLE (gt 50) (triangle 50 "solid" "green"))`

`(define (gt size) (gt size "solid" "green"))`

Highlight and label the variables in the example lists below. Then, using `gt` as a model, match the examples to their corresponding function definitions.

Examples			Definition

`(EXAMPLE (f "solid")`
`  (circle 8 "solid" "red"))`
`(EXAMPLE (f "outline")`
`  (circle 8 "outline" "red"))`
	1	A	`(define (f s) (star s "outline" "red"))`

`(EXAMPLE (f 2) (+ 2 2))`
`(EXAMPLE (f 4) (+ 4 4))`
`(EXAMPLE (f 5) (+ 5 5))`
	2	B	`(define (f num) (+ num num))`

`(EXAMPLE (f "red") (circle 7 "solid" "red"))`
`(EXAMPLE (f "teal")`
`  (circle 7 "solid" "teal"))`
	3	C	`(define (f c) (star 9 "solid" c))`

`(EXAMPLE (f "red") (star 9 "solid" "red"))`
`(EXAMPLE (f "grey") (star 9 "solid" "grey"))`
`(EXAMPLE (f "pink") (star 9 "solid" "pink"))`
	4	D	`(define (f s) (circle 8 s "red"))`

`(EXAMPLE (f 3) (star 3 "outline" "red"))` `(EXAMPLE (f 8) (star 8 "outline" "red"))`	5	E	`(define (f c) (circle 7 "solid" c))`

Creating Contracts From Examples

Write the contracts used to create each of the following collections of examples.

1) _____

```
(EXAMPLE (big-triangle 100 "red")
  (triangle 100 "solid" "red"))
(EXAMPLE (big-triangle 200 "orange")
  (triangle 200 "solid" "orange"))
```

2) _____

```
(EXAMPLE (purple-square 15)
  (rectangle 15 15 "outline" "purple"))
(EXAMPLE (purple-square 6)
  (rectangle 6 6 "outline" "purple"))
```

3) _____

```
(EXAMPLE (banner "Game Today!")
  (text "Game Today!" 50 "red"))
(EXAMPLE (banner "Go Team!")
  (text "Go Team!" 50 "red"))
(EXAMPLE (banner "Exit")
  (text "Exit" 50 "red"))
```

4) _____

```
(EXAMPLE (twinkle "outline" "red")
  (star 5 "outline" "red"))
(EXAMPLE (twinkle "solid" "pink")
  (star 5 "solid" "pink"))
(EXAMPLE (twinkle "outline" "grey")
  (star 5 "outline" "grey"))
```

5) _____

```
(EXAMPLE (half 5) (/ 5 2))
(EXAMPLE (half 8) (/ 8 2))
(EXAMPLE (half 900) (/ 900 2))
```

Contracts, Examples & Definitions - bc

gt

Directions: Define a function called `gt`, which makes solid green triangles of whatever size we want.

Every contract has three parts...

; gt : _____ Number _____ -> Image
  function name   *Domain*   *Range*

Write some examples, then circle and label what changes...

(EXAMPLE (gt _____ 10 _____) (triangle 10 "solid" "green") _____)
            function name   *input(s)*   *what the function produces*

(EXAMPLE (gt _____ 20 _____) (triangle 20 "solid" "green") _____)
            function name   *input(s)*   *what the function produces*

Write the definition, giving variable names to all your input values...

(define (gt _____ size _____)
          function name   *variable(s)*

  (triangle size "solid" "green") _____)
              what the function does with those variable(s)

bc

Directions: Define a function called `bc`, which makes solid blue circles of whatever radius we want.

Every contract has three parts...

; _____ : _____ -> _____
  function name   *Domain*   *Range*

Write some examples, then circle and label what changes...

(EXAMPLE (_____) _____)
            function name *input(s)*   *what the function produces*

(EXAMPLE (_____) _____)
            function name *input(s)*   *what the function produces*

Write the definition, giving variable names to all your input values...

(define (_____)
          function name   *variable(s)*

  _____)
     what the function does with those variable(s)

62

sticker

Directions: Define a function called `sticker`, which consumes a color and draws a 50px star of the given color.

Every contract has three parts...

; _____ : _____ -> _____
      function name   *Domain*   *Range*

Write some examples, then circle and label what changes...

(EXAMPLE (_____) _____)
            function name   *input(s)*   *what the function produces*

(EXAMPLE (_____) _____)
            function name   *input(s)*   *what the function produces*

Write the definition, giving variable names to all your input values...

(define (_____)
                function name   *variable(s)*

_____)
               what the function does with those variable(s)

gold-star

Directions: Define a function called `gold-star`, which takes in a number and draws a solid gold star of that given size.

Every contract has three parts...

; _____ : _____ -> _____
      function name   *Domain*   *Range*

Write some examples, then circle and label what changes...

(EXAMPLE (_____) _____)
            function name   *input(s)*   *what the function produces*

(EXAMPLE (_____) _____)
            function name   *input(s)*   *what the function produces*

Write the definition, giving variable names to all your input values...

(define (_____)
                function name   *variable(s)*

_____)
               what the function does with those variable(s)

Contracts, Examples & Definitions - Name

name-color

Directions: Define a function called `name-color`, which makes an image of your name at size 50 in whatever color is given.

Every contract has three parts...

: _____ : _____ -> _____
  function name   Domain   Range

Write some examples, then circle and label what changes...

(EXAMPLE (_____) _____)
              function name   input(s)   what the function produces

(EXAMPLE (_____) _____)
              function name   input(s)   what the function produces

Write the definition, giving variable names to all your input values...

(define (_____)
              function name   variable(s)

_____)
                        what the function does with those variable(s)

name-size

Directions: Define a function called `name-size`, which makes an image of your name in your favorite color (be sure to specify your name and favorite color!) in whatever size is given.

Every contract has three parts...

: _____ : _____ -> _____
  function name   Domain   Range

Write some examples, then circle and label what changes...

(EXAMPLE (_____) _____)
              function name   input(s)   what the function produces

(EXAMPLE (_____) _____)
              function name   input(s)   what the function produces

Write the definition, giving variable names to all your input values...

(define (_____)
              function name   variable(s)

_____)
                        what the function does with those variable(s)

What's on your mind?

Notice and Wonder (Linearity)

Part 1:

x	y
0	0
1	2
2	4
3	6
4	8

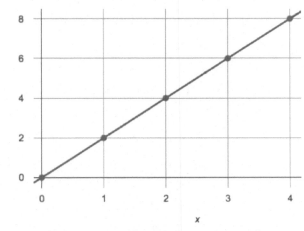

What do you Notice?	What do you Wonder?

Part 2:

- What would be the next (x,y) pair for each of the tables?
- What would the y-value for each table be when x is 0?

x	y
0	
1	2
2	3
3	4
4	5
5	6

x	y
0	
1	20
2	17
3	14
4	11
5	8

For each of the tables below, find the graph that matches.

Note: Scales on the graphs vary. The tables are shown sideways to save space.

x	1	2	3	4	5
y	4	5	6	7	8

1

A

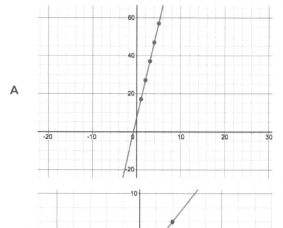

x	-5	-4	-3	-2	-1
y	5	4	3	2	1

2

B

x	1	2	3	4	5
y	17	27	37	47	57

3

C

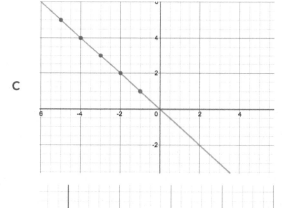

x	-2	-1	0	1	2
y	-6	-3	0	3	6

4

D

Are All Graphs Linear?

If all linear relationships can be shown as points on a graph, does that mean all graphs are linear?

Beneath each graph write **linear** or **not linear**.

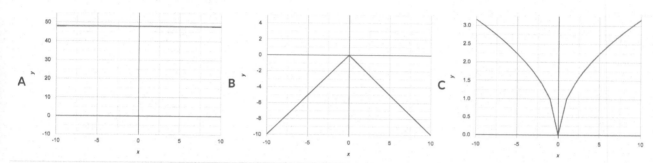

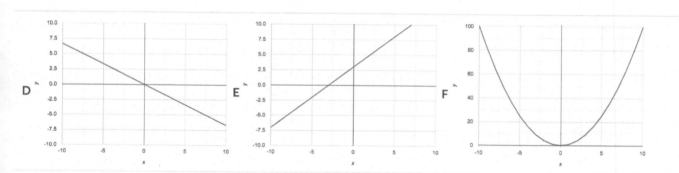

What do you Notice?	What do you Wonder?

Are All Tables Linear?

If all linear relationships can be shown as tables, does that mean all tables are linear? Look at the six tables shown below.

1) Extend as many of the tables as you can by adding the next (x,y) pair in the sequence.

2) If the table is linear, write down your prediction of what the y-value will be when x = 0.

3) If the table is not linear, write **not linear** instead of the y-intercept.

A

x	-2	-1	0	1	2	
y	-2	-3	-4	-5	-6	

when x=0, y will equal _____

B

x	2	3	4	5	6	
y	-12	-14	-16	-18	-20	

when x=0, y will equal _____

C

x	1	2	3	4	5	
y	1	4	9	16	25	

when x=0, y will equal _____

D

x	5	6	7	8	9	
y	3	3	3	3	3	

when x=0, y will equal _____

E

x	1	2	3	4	5	
y	84	94	104	114	124	

when x=0, y will equal _____

F

x	-10	-9	-8	-7	-6	
y	$\frac{-1}{10}$	$\frac{-1}{9}$	$\frac{-1}{8}$	$\frac{-1}{7}$	$\frac{-1}{6}$	

when x=0, y will equal _____

What do you Notice?	What do you Wonder?

Linear, Non-linear, or Bust?

Decide whether each representation is of a linear function, a non-linear function or is not a function at all!

Remember: Functions will pass the Vertical Line Test!

1

x	y
1	5
2	10
3	15
4	20
5	25
6	30
7	35

Linear   Non-Linear   Not a Function

2

Linear   Non-Linear   Not a Function

3

Linear   Non-Linear   Not a Function

4

x	y
1	1
2	4
3	9
4	16
5	25
6	36
7	49

Linear   Non-Linear   Not a Function

5

x	y
1	1
2	2
3	3
4	4
4	5
6	6
7	9

Linear   Non-Linear   Not a Function

6

Linear   Non-Linear   Not a Function

slope (rate): *how much y changes as x-increases by 1*

y-intercept: *the y-value when $x = 0$*

x	-1	0	1	2	3	4
y	-1	1	3	5	7	9

1) Compute the slope: _____

2) Compute the y-intercept: _____

3) What strategies did you use to compute the slope and y-intercept?

_____

_____

The slope and y-intercept in this table are harder to find, because the x-values don't go up by 1 and we can't see a value for $x = 0$. **Try filling in the points that have been skipped to Compute the slope and y-intercept.**

x	2	5	8	11
y	3	9	15	21

4) Compute the slope: 2 _____

5) Compute the y-intercept: _____

The slope and y-intercept in this table are even harder to find, because the x-values are out of order!

Calculate the slope and y-intercept from *any* two points! Be sure to show your work.

x	3	20	5	9	1
y	5	56	11	23	-1

6) Compute the slope: _____

7) Compute the y-intercept: _____

Slope & y-Intercept from Tables (Basic Practice)

x	-1	0	1	2	3	4
y	-1	2	5	8	11	14

1) slope: _____ y-intercept: _____

x	-2	-1	0	1	2	3
y	15	10	5	0	-5	-10

2) slope: _____ y-intercept: _____

x	-3	-2	-1	0	1	2
y	-1	-0.5	0	0.5	1	1.5

3) slope: _____ y-intercept: _____

x	-1	0	1	2	3	4
y	-7	-3	1	5	9	13

4) slope: _____ y-intercept: _____

x	-5	-4	-3	-2	-1	0
y	1	2.5	4	5.5	7	8.5

5) slope: _____ y-intercept: _____

x	-3	-2	-1	0	1	2
y	0	12.5	25	37.5	50	62.5

6) slope: _____ y-intercept: _____

x	1	2	3	4	5	6
y	5	3	1	-1	-3	-5

7) slope: _____ y-intercept: _____

x	-4	-2	0	2	4	6
y	0	4	8	12	16	20

8) slope: _____ y-intercept: _____

Can you identify the **slope** for the functions represented in each of these tables?

Note: Some tables may have their rows out of order!

	x	y
	0	3
1	1	5
	2	7
	3	9

slope/rate: _____

	x	y
	-5	35
2	-4	28
	-3	21
	-2	14

slope/rate: _____

	x	y
	12	15
3	13	15.5
	14	16
	16	17

slope/rate: _____

	x	y
	1	39
4	4	36
	3	37
	2	38

slope/rate: _____

	x	y
	13	57
5	9	41
	11	49
	7	33

slope/rate: _____

Identifying Slope and y-intercept in Graphs

Can you identify the **slope** and **y-intercept** for each of these graphs?

1

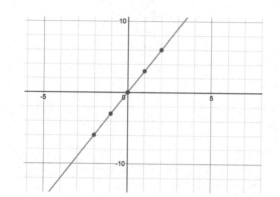

slope/rate: _____

y-intercept: _____

2

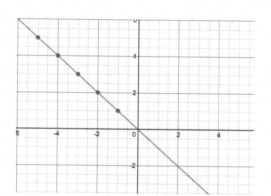

slope/rate: _____

y-intercept: _____

3

slope/rate: _____

y-intercept: _____

4

slope/rate: _____

y-intercept: _____

Solving Word Problems

Being able to see functions as Contracts, Examples or Definitions is like having three powerful tools. These representations can be used together to solve word problems!

1) When reading a word problem, the first step is to figure out the **Contract** for the function you want to build. Remember, a Contract must include the Name, Domain and Range for the function!

2) Then we write a **Purpose Statement**, which is a short note that tells us what the function *should do*. Professional programmers work hard to write good purpose statements, so that other people can understand the code they wrote!

3) Next, we write at least two **Examples**. These are lines of code that show what the function should do for a *specific* input. Once we see examples of at least two inputs, we can *find a pattern* and see which parts are changing and which parts aren't.

4) To finish the Examples, we circle the parts that are changing, and label them with a short **variable name** that explains what they do.

5) Finally, we **define the function** itself! This is pretty easy after you have some examples to work from: we copy everything that didn't change, and replace the changeable stuff with the variable name!

Matching Word Problems and Purpose Statements

Match each word problem below to its corresponding purpose statement.

1	Annie got a new dog, Xavier, that eats about 5 times as much as her little dog, Rex, who is 10 years old. She hasn't gotten used to buying enough dogfood for the household yet. Write a function that generates an estimate for how many pounds of food Xavier will eat, given the amount of food that Rex usually consumes in the same amount of time.	A	Consume the pounds of food Rex eats and add 5.
2	Adrienne's raccoon, Rex, eats 5 more pounds of food each week than her pet squirrel, Lili, who is 7 years older. Write a function to determine how much Lili eats in a week, given how much Rex eats.	B	Consume the pounds of food Rex eats and subtract 5.
3	Alejandro's rabbit, Rex, poops about 1/5 of what it eats. His rabbit hutch is 10 cubic feet. Write a function to figure out how much rabbit poop Alejandro will have to clean up depending on how much Rex has eaten.	C	Consume the pounds of food Rex eats and multiply by 5.
4	Max's turtle, Rex, eats 5 pounds less per week than his turtle, Harry, who is 2 inches taller. Write a function to calculate how much food Harry eats, given the weight of Rex's food.	D	Consume the pounds of food Rex eats and divide by 5.

Writing Examples from Purpose Statements

We've provided contracts and purpose statements to describe two different functions. Write examples for each of those functions.

Contract and Purpose Statement

Every contract has three parts...

; triple **:** _____ Number _____ -> Number
    function name   *Domain*   *Range*

; Consumes a Number and triples it.
                         what does the function do?

Examples

Write some examples, then circle and label what changes...

(EXAMPLE (_____) _____)
         function name   *input(s)*   *what the function produces*

(EXAMPLE (_____) _____)
         function name   *input(s)*   *what the function produces*

Contract and Purpose Statement

Every contract has three parts...

; upside-down: _____ Image _____ -> Image
    function name   *Domain*   *Range*

; Consumes an image, and turns it upside down by rotating it 180 degrees.
                         what does the function do?

Examples

Write some examples, then circle and label what changes...

(EXAMPLE (_____)
         function name   *input(s)*

_____)
             what the function produces

(EXAMPLE (_____) _____)
         function name   *input(s)*   *what the function produces*

Fixing Purpose Statements

Beneath each of the word problems below is a purpose statement that is either missing information or includes unnecessary information. Write an improved version of each purpose statement beneath the original.

1) **Word Problem:** *The New York City ferry costs $2.75 per ride. The Earth School Requires two chaperones for any field trip. Write a function* `fare` *that takes in the number of students in the class and returns the total fare for the students and chaperones.*

Purpose Statement: Define a function `fare` to take in the number of students and add 2.

Improved Purpose Statement:

_____

_____

_____

_____

2) **Word Problem:** *It is tradition for the Green Machines to go to Humpy Dumpty's for ice cream with their families after their soccer games. Write a function* `cones` *to take in the number of kids and calculate the total bill for the team, assuming that each kid brings two family members and cones cost $1.25.*

Purpose Statement: Define a function `cones` to take in the number of kids on the team and multiply it by 1.25.

Improved Purpose Statement:

_____

_____

_____

_____

3) **Word Problem:** *The cost of renting an ebike is $3 plus an additional $0.12 per minute. Write a function* `ebike` *that will calculate the cost of a ride, given the number of minutes ridden.*

Purpose Statement: Define a function `ebike` to take in the number of minutes and multiply it by 3.12.

Improved Purpose Statement:

_____

_____

_____

_____

4) **Word Problem:** *Suleika is a skilled house painter at only age 21. She has painted hundreds of rooms and can paint about 175 square feet an hour. Write a function* `paint` *that takes in the number of square feet of the job and calculates how many hours it will take her.*

Purpose Statement: Define a function `paint` to take in the number of square feet of walls in a house and divide them by 175 to calculate the number of hours that it will take 21 year-old Suleika to complete the paint job.

Improved Purpose Statement:

_____

_____

_____

_____

Word Problem: rocket-height

Directions: A rocket blasts off, and is now traveling at a constant velocity of 7 meters per second. Use the Design Recipe to write a function `rocket-height`, which takes in a number of seconds and calculates the height.

Contract and Purpose Statement

Every contract has three parts...

; _____ : _____ -> _____
      function name   *Domain*   *Range*

; _____
                what does the function do?

Examples

Write some examples, then circle and label what changes...

(EXAMPLE (_____) _____)
         function name   *input(s)*   *what the function produces*

(EXAMPLE (_____) _____)
         function name   *input(s)*   *what the function produces*

Definition

Write the definition, giving variable names to all your input values...

(define (_____)
        function name   *variable(s)*

_____)
            what the function does with those variable(s)

Danger and Target Movement

Directions: Use the Design Recipe to write a function `update-danger` , which takes in the danger's x-coordinate and produces the next x-coordinate, which is 50 pixels to the left.

Contract and Purpose Statement

Every contract has three parts...

: _____ : _____ -> _____
    function name   *Domain*   *Range*

: _____
                         what does the function do?

Examples

Write some examples, then circle and label what changes...

(EXAMPLE (_____) _____)
              function name   *input(s)*   *what the function produces*

(EXAMPLE (_____) _____)
              function name   *input(s)*   *what the function produces*

Definition

Write the definition, giving variable names to all your input values...

(define (_____)
              function name   *variable(s)*
)

_____
                         what the function does with those variable(s)

Directions: Use the Design Recipe to write a function `update-target` , which takes in the target's x-coordinate and produces the next x-coordinate, which is 50 pixels to the right.

Contract and Purpose Statement

Every contract has three parts...

: _____ : _____ -> _____
    function name   *Domain*   *Range*

: _____
                         what does the function do?

Examples

Write some examples, then circle and label what changes...

(EXAMPLE (_____) _____)
              function name   *input(s)*   *what the function produces*

(EXAMPLE (_____) _____)
               function name   *input(s)*   *what the function produces*

Definition

Write the definition, giving variable names to all your input values...

(define (_____)
              function name   *variable(s)*
)

_____
                         what the function does with those variable(s)

Surface Area of a Rectangular Prism - Explore

1) What do you picture in your mind when you hear *rectangular prism*?

_____

_____

2) What do you picture in your mind when you hear *surface area*?

_____

_____

3) Open the <u>Surface Area of a Rectangular Prism Starter File</u> and click "Run".

4) Type `prism` into the Interactions Area and hit "enter" to see an image of a rectangular prism. What do you notice about the image?

_____

_____

5) How many faces does this prism have?   _____

Find PART 1 in the starter file. You will see a definition for `front` and `back`.

6) How did the author know to use width and height as the dimensions for `front` and `back`?

_____

_____

7) Why are `front` and `back` defined to be the same thing?

_____

_____

8) Add definitions for the other faces of the prism, using these definitions as a model, and the image of the prism as a support.

Find PART 2 in the starter file. You'll see a list that only includes `front` and `back`.

9) Complete the faces list, then type (`print-imgs faces`) into the interactions area.} What do you see?

_____

_____

We're going to print the faces following directions in PART 3 and build a paper model of a rectangular prism.

Before you print and build your prism, you can change the length, width, and height of your prism at the top of the starter file. Be sure that all 3 dimensions are different, and that they are all small enough to fit on a sheet of paper. If you change them, record your new dimensions here.

LENGTH: _____ WIDTH: _____ HEIGHT: _____

12) Calculate the surface area of your prism, by adding the area of each face. _____ Show your work below.

13) In PART 4 of the starter file, you wrote code to calculate the surface area. How many definitions did you use? _____

14) How does the surface area that the computer returns compare to the surface area you calculated by hand?

_____

Problem Decomposition

- Sometimes a problem is too complicated to solve all at once. Maybe there are too many variables, or there is just so much information that we can't get a handle on it!
- We can use **Problem Decomposition** to break those problems down into simpler pieces, and then work with the pieces to solve the whole. There are two strategies we can use for decomposition:
  - **Top-Down** - Start with the "big picture", writing functions or equations that describe the connections between parts of the problem. Then, work on defining those parts.
  - **Bottom-Up** - Start with the smaller parts, writing functions or equations that describe the parts we understand. Then, connect those parts together to solve the whole problem.
- You may find that one strategy works better for some types of problems than another, so make sure you're comfortable using either one!

Word Problems: revenue, cost

Directions: Use the Design Recipe to write a function `revenue`, which takes in the number of glasses sold at $1.75 apiece and calculates the total revenue.

Contract and Purpose Statement

Every contract has three parts...

: _____ : _____ -> _____
   function name   *Domain*   *Range*

: _____
            what does the function do?

Examples

Write some examples, then circle and label what changes...

(EXAMPLE (_____) _____)
       function name   *input(s)*   *what the function produces*

(EXAMPLE (_____) _____)
       function name   *input(s)*   *what the function produces*

Definition

Write the definition, giving variable names to all your input values...

(define (_____)
        function name   *variable(s)*

_____)
          what the function does with those variable(s)

Directions: Use the Design Recipe to write a function `cost`, which takes in the number of glasses sold and calculates the total cost of materials if each glass costs $.30 to make.

Contract and Purpose Statement

Every contract has three parts...

: _____ : _____ -> _____
   function name   *Domain*   *Range*

: _____
            what does the function do?

Examples

Write some examples, then circle and label what changes...

(EXAMPLE (_____) _____)
       function name   *input(s)*   *what the function produces*

(EXAMPLE (_____) _____)
       function name   *input(s)*   *what the function produces*

Definition

Write the definition, giving variable names to all your input values...

(define (_____)
        function name   *variable(s)*

_____)
          what the function does with those variable(s)

Word Problem: profit

Directions: Use the Design Recipe to write a function `profit` that calculates total profit from glasses sold, which is computed by subtracting the total cost from the total revenue.

Contract and Purpose Statement

Every contract has three parts...

; _____ : _____ -> _____
       function name   Domain   Range

; _____
                      what does the function do?

Examples

Write some examples, then circle and label what changes...

(EXAMPLE (_____) _____)
                 function name   input(s)   what the function produces

(EXAMPLE (_____) _____)
                 function name   input(s)   what the function produces

Definition

Write the definition, giving variable names to all your input values...

(define (_____)
                 function name   variable(s)

   _____)
                      what the function does with those variable(s)

Profit - More than one Way!

Four students defined the same `revenue` and `cost` functions, shown below:

```
(define (revenue g) (* 1.75 g))
(define (cost g) (* 0.3 g))
```

However, they came up with **four different definitions** for `profit` :

Khalil:	`(define (profit g) (- (* 1.75 g) (* 0.3 g)))`
Samaria:	`(define (profit g) (* (- 1.75 0.3) g))`
Alenka:	`(define (profit g) (* 1.45 g))`
Fauzi:	`(define (profit g) (- (revenue g) (cost g)))`

1) Which of these four definitions do you think is "best", and why?

_____

_____

_____

_____

2) If lemons get more expensive, which definitions of `profit` need to be changed?

_____

_____

_____

3) If Sally raises her prices, which definitions of `profit` need to be changed?

_____

_____

_____

4) Which definition of `profit` is the most flexible? Why?

_____

_____

_____

_____

Top Down or Bottom Up

Jamal's trip requires him to drive 20mi to the airport, fly 2,300mi, and then take a bus 6mi to his hotel. His average speed driving to the airport is 40mph, the average speed of an airplane is 575mph, and the average speed of his bus is 15mph.

Aside from time waiting for the plane or bus, how long is Jamal in transit?

Bear's Strategy:	Lion's Strategy:
$DriveTime = 20miles \times \dfrac{1\,hour}{40miles} = 0.5\,hours$	$InTransitTime = DriveTime + FlyTime + BusTime$
$FlyTime = 2300miles \times \dfrac{1\,hour}{575miles} = 4\,hours$	$DriveTime = 20miles \times \dfrac{1\,hour}{40miles} = 0.5\,hours$
$BusTime = 6miles \times \dfrac{1\,hour}{15miles} = 0.4\,hours$	$FlyTime = 2300miles \times \dfrac{1\,hour}{575miles} = 4\,hours$
$InTransitTime = DriveTime + FlyTime + BusTime$	$BusTime = 6miles \times \dfrac{1\,hour}{15miles} = 0.4\,hours$
$0.5 + 4 + 0.4 = 4.9\,hours$	$0.5 + 4 + 0.4 = 4.9\,hours$

1) Whose Strategy was Top Down? How do you know?

2) Whose Strategy was Bottom Up? How do you know?

3) Which way of thinking about the problem makes more sense to you?

What's happening with that Math?!

Setting up the problem so that the units will cancel out helps us to know whether to divide or multiply! In this case, in order to cancel out the miles, 40 miles has to go on the bottom, so we end up dividing by 40.

$$\frac{20mi}{1} \times \frac{1hr}{40mi} = \frac{20\,\cancel{mi} \times 1hr}{40\,\cancel{mi}} = \frac{20hr}{40} = 20 \div 40 = 0.5\,hrs$$

Inequalities

- Sometimes we want to *ask questions* about data. For example, is `x` greater than `y`? Is one string equal to another? These questions can't be answered with **Numbers**. Instead, they are answered with a new data type called a **Boolean**.

- video games use Booleans for many things: asking when a player's health is equal to zero, whether two characters are close enough to bump into one another, or if a character's coordinates put it off the edge of the screen.

- A Boolean value is either `true` or `false`. Unlike Numbers, Strings, and Images, Booleans have only two possible values.

- You already know some functions that produce Booleans, such as `<` and `>`! Our programming language has them, too: `(< 3 4)`, `(> 10 2)`, and `(= -10 19)`.

- We also have ways of writing **Compound Inequalities**, so we can ask more complicated questions using the **and** and **or** functions.

  - `(and (> 3 4) (< 10 2))` translates to "three is greater than four *and* ten is less than two". This will evaluate to `false`, since the **and** function requires that both sub-expressions be `true`.

  - `(or (> 3 4) (< 10 2))`, which translates to "three is greater than four *or* ten is less than two". This will evaluate to `true`, since the **or** function only requires that one sub-expression be `true`.

- The Circles of Evaluation work the same way with Booleans that they do with Numbers, Strings and Images:

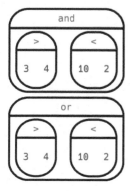

Boolean Functions

Explore the functions in the *Booleans Starter File* . What characteristics define them as Booleans?

_____

_____

_____

Fill in the blanks below so that each of the five functions returns `true`

1) (odd? _____)

2) (even? _____)

3) (less-than-one? _____)

4) (continent? _____)

5) (primary-color? _____)

Fill in the blanks below so that each of the five functions returns `false`

6) (odd? _____)

7) (even? _____)

8) (less-than-one? _____)

9) (continent? _____)

10) (primary-color? _____)

Simple Inequalities

Each inequality expression in the first column contains a number.

Decide whether or not that number is a solution to the expression and place it in the appropriate column.

Then identify 4 *solution* and 4 *non-solution* values for `x` .

- **Solutions** will make the expression `true` .

- **Non-Solutions** will make the expression `false` .

Challenge yourself to use negatives, positives, fractions, decimals, etc. for your `x` values.

	Expression	4 solutions that evaluate to `true`	4 non-solutions that evaluate to `false`
a	`(> x 2)`		
b	`(<= x -2)`		
c	`(< x 3.5)`		
d	`(>= x -1)`		
e	`(> x -4)`		
f	`(<> x 2)`		

1) For which inequalities was the number from the expression part of the solution?

_____

2) For which inequalities was the number from the expression not part of the solution?

_____

3) For which inequalities were the solutions on the left end of the number line?

_____

4) For which inequalities were the solutions on the right end of the number line?

_____

Converting Circles of Evaluation to Code

For each Circle of Evaluation on the left-hand side, write the Code for the Circle on the right-hand side

	Circle of Evaluation	Code
1	> (+ (4 5) 9)	
2	and (< (5 10) < (10 15))	
3	or (string=? (yum "apple") string=? (yum "banana"))	
4	>= (string-length ("My Game") 6)	
5	or (and (< (1 x) < (x 5)) and (< (8 x) < (x 10)))	

Create the Circles of Evaluation, then convert the expressions into Code in the space provided.

1) 2 is less than 5, and 0 is equal to 6

What will this evaluate to? _____

2) 6 is greater than 8, or -4 is less than 1

What will this evaluate to? _____

3) The String "purple" is the same as the String "blue", and 3 plus 5 equals 8

What will this evaluate to? _____

4) Write the contracts for **and** & **or** in your Contracts page.

Compound Inequalities: Solutions & Non-Solutions

For each Compound Inequality listed below, identify 4 *solutions* and 4 *non-solutions*.

If there are **no solutions** or the solution set includes **all real numbers**, write that instead of making a list.

- Solutions for *intersections*, which use **and** will make both of the expressions `true`.
- Solutions for *unions*, which use **or** will make at least one of the expressions `true`.

Pay special attention to the numbers in the sample expression! Challenge yourself to use negatives, positives, fractions, decimals, etc. for your `x` values.

The first two have been done for you - Answers will vary!

	Expression	4 solutions that evaluate to `true`	4 non-solutions that evaluate to `false`
a	x > 5 and x < 15	6, 9.5, 12, 14.9	-2, 5, 15, 16.1
b	x > 5 or x < 15	All real numbers	No non-solutions
c	x <= -2 and x > 7		
d	x <= -2 or x > 7		
e	x < 3.5 and x > -4		
f	x < 3.5 or x > -4		
g	x >= -1 and x > -5		
h	x >= -1 or x > -5		
i	x < -4 and x > 2		

1) Could there ever be a union with *no solutions*? Explain your thinking.

_____

_____

_____

2) Could there ever be an intersection whose solution is *all real numbers*? Explain your thinking.

_____

_____

_____

Compound Inequality Functions

Each of the plots below was generated using the code `inequality(comp-ineq, [list: -1, 0, 1.6, 3, 5.2, 7, 8.1, 9] )`.
Using the numbers 3 and 7, write the code to define `comp-ineq` for each plot. *Note: The example is defined using 0 and 8.1 rather than 3 and 7.*

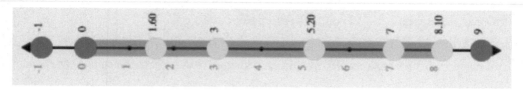

code: `(define (comp-ineq x) (and (> x 0) (<= x 8.1)))`

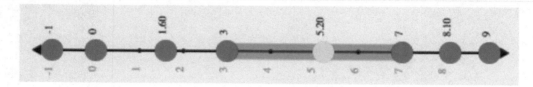

code: _____

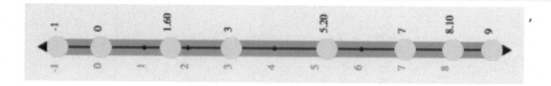

code: _____

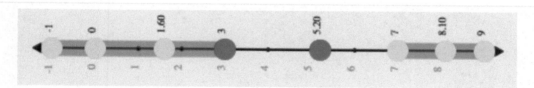

code: _____

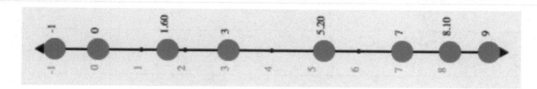

code: _____

Sam the Butterfly

Open the "Sam the Butterfly" starter file and click "Run". *(Hi, Sam!)*

Move Sam around the screen using the arrow keys.

1) What do you Notice about the program?

_____

_____

2) What do you Wonder?

_____

_____

3) What do you see when Sam is at (0,0)? Why is that?

_____

4) What changes as the butterfly moves left and right?

_____

Sam is in a 640 × 480 yard. Sam's mom wants Sam to stay in sight. **How far to the left and right can Sam go and still remain visible?**

_____

_____

Use the new inequality functions to answer the following questions *with code*:

5) Sam hasn't gone off the left edge of the screen as long as... _____

6) Sam hasn't gone off the right edge of the screen as long as... _____

7) Use the space below to draw Circles of Evaluation for these two expressions:

Left and Right

Directions: Use the Design Recipe to write a function `safe-left?`, which takes in an x-coordinate and checks to see if it is greater than -50.

Contract and Purpose Statement

Every contract has three parts...

; _____ : _____ -> _____
     function name   Domain   Range

; _____
                   what does the function do?

Examples

Write some examples, then circle and label what changes...

(EXAMPLE (_____) _____)
           function name   input(s)   what the function produces

(EXAMPLE (_____) _____)
           function name   input(s)   what the function produces

Definition

Write the definition, giving variable names to all your input values...

(define (_____)
        function name   variable(s)

_____)
           what the function does with those variable(s)

Directions: Use the Design Recipe to write a function `safe-right?`, which takes in an x-coordinate and checks to see if it is less than 690.

Contract and Purpose Statement

Every contract has three parts...

; _____ : _____ -> _____
     function name   Domain   Range

; _____
                   what does the function do?

Examples

Write some examples, then circle and label what changes...

(EXAMPLE (_____) _____)
           function name   input(s)   what the function produces

(EXAMPLE (_____) _____)
           function name   input(s)   what the function produces

Definition

Write the definition, giving variable names to all your input values...

(define (_____)
        function name   variable(s)

_____)
           what the function does with those variable(s)

Word Problem: onscreen?

Directions: Use the Design Recipe to write a function `onscreen?`, which takes in an x-coordinate and checks to see if Sam is safe on the left while also being safe on the right.

Contract and Purpose Statement ☐

Every contract has three parts...

; _____ : _____ -> _____
  function name   Domain   Range

; _____
                        what does the function do?

Examples ☐

Write some examples, then circle and label what changes...

(EXAMPLE (_____) _____)
              function name   input(s)   what the function produces

(EXAMPLE (_____) _____)
              function name   input(s)   what the function produces

Definition ☐

Write the definition, giving variable names to all your input values...

(define (_____)
             function name   variable(s)

_____)
                  what the function does with those variable(s)

Piecewise Functions

- Sometimes we want to build functions that act differently for different inputs. For example, suppose a business charges $10/pizza, but only $5 for orders of six or more. How could we write a function that computes the total price based on the number of pizzas?

- In math, **Piecewise Functions** are functions that can behave one way for part of their Domain, and another way for a different part. In our pizza example, our function would act like $cost(pizzas) = 10 * pizzas$ for anywhere from 1-5 pizzas. But after 5, it acts like $cost(pizzas) = 5 * pizzas$.

- Piecewise functions are divided into "pieces". Each piece is divided into two parts:

  1. How the function should behave

  2. The domain where it behaves that way

- Our programming language can be used to write piecewise functions, too! Just as in math, each piece has two parts:
  ```
  (define (cost pizzas)
    (cond
      [(>= pizzas 6) (* 5 pizzas)])
  ```

Piecewise functions are powerful, and let us solve more complex problems. We can use piecewise functions in a video game to add or subtract from a character's x-coordinate, moving it left or right depending on which key was pressed.

1) Open the Red Shape Starter File, and read through the code you find there. This code contains new programming that you haven't seen yet! Take a moment to list everything you Notice, and then everything you Wonder...

Notice	Wonder

2) What happens if you click "Run" and type (red-shape "ellipse") ?

_____

3) Add **another example** for "triangle".

4) Add another line of code to the definition, to define what the function should do with the input "triangle".

5) Come up with some new shapes, and add them to the code. Make sure you include examples or you will get an error message!

6) In your own words, describe how *piecewise functions* work in this programming environment.

_____

_____

_____

_____

Word Problem: red-shape

Directions: A friend loves red shapes so we've decided to write a program that makes it easy to generate them. Write a function called `red-shape` which takes in the name of a shape and makes a 20-pixel, solid, red image of the shape.

Contract and Purpose Statement

Every contract has three parts...

`;` red-shape :   String   -> Image

      function name   *Domain*   *Range*

`;` Given a shape name, produce a solid, red, 20-pixel image of the shape.

                                                what does the function do?

Examples

Write some examples, then circle and label what changes...

(EXAMPLE (red-shape   "circle"   ) (circle 20 "solid" "red")   )

            function name   *input(s)*   *what the function produces*

(EXAMPLE (red-shape   "triangle"   ) (triangle 20 "solid" "red")   )

            function name   *input(s)*   *what the function produces*

(EXAMPLE (red-shape   "rectangle"   ) (rectangle 20 20 "solid" "red")   )

            function name   *input(s)*   *what the function produces*

(EXAMPLE (red-shape   "star"   ) (star 20 "solid" "red")   )

            function name   *input(s)*   *what the function produces*

Definition

Write the definition, giving variable names to all your input values...

(define (   )

            function name   *variable(s)*

   (cond

      [   ]

      [   ]

      [   ]

      [   ]

      [

                                      ]   ))

Word Problem: update-player

Directions: The player moves by 20 pixels each time the up or down key is pressed. Write a function called `update-player`, which takes in the player's y-coordinate and the name of the key pressed ("up" or "down"), and returns the new y-coordinate.

Contract and Purpose Statement

Every contract has three parts...

; _____ : _____ -> _____
     function name   *Domain*   *Range*

; _____
                                  what does the function do?

Examples

Write some examples, then circle and label what changes...

(EXAMPLE (update-player   300   "up"   ) _____)
                 function name   *input(s)*   *what the function produces*

(EXAMPLE (_____) _____)
                 function name   *input(s)*   *what the function produces*

(EXAMPLE (_____) _____)
                 function name   *input(s)*   *what the function produces*

(EXAMPLE (_____) _____)
                 function name   *input(s)*   *what the function produces*

Definition

Write the definition, giving variable names to all your input values...

(define (_____)
                 function name   *variable(s)*

  (cond _____

    [_____   _____]

    [_____   _____]

    [_____   _____]))

Challenges for update-player

For each of the challenges below, see if you can come up with two EXAMPLEs of how it should work!

1) Warping - Program one key to "warp" the player to a set location, such as the center of the screen.

(EXAMPLE (update-player _____ _____)

_____)

(EXAMPLE (update-player _____ _____)

_____)

2) Boundaries - Change `update-player` such that `PLAYER` cannot move off the top or bottom of the screen.

(EXAMPLE (update-player _____ _____)

_____)

(EXAMPLE (update-player _____ _____)

_____)

3) Wrapping - Add code to `update-player` such that when `PLAYER` moves to the top of the screen, it reappears at the bottom, and vice versa.

(EXAMPLE (update-player _____ _____)

_____)

(EXAMPLE (update-player _____ _____)

_____)

4) Hiding - Add a key that will make `PLAYER` seem to disappear, and reappear when the same key is pressed again.

(EXAMPLE (update-player _____ _____)

_____)

(EXAMPLE (update-player _____ _____)

_____)

Writing Code to Calculate Missing Lengths

In each of the game screenshots below, one of the distance labels has been hidden. Write the code to generate the missing distance on the line below each image. *Hint: Remember the Pythagorean Theorem!*

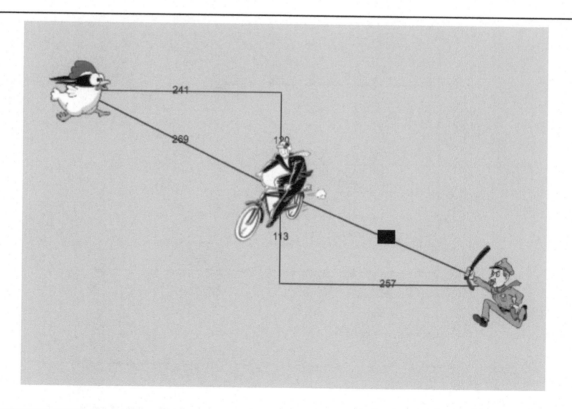

Distance between the pyret and the boot:

```
(sqrt (+ (sqr (line-length 9 -3)) (sqr (line-length 3 -2))))
```

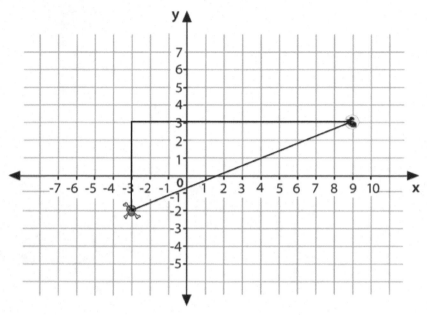

Explain how the code works. _____

_____

_____

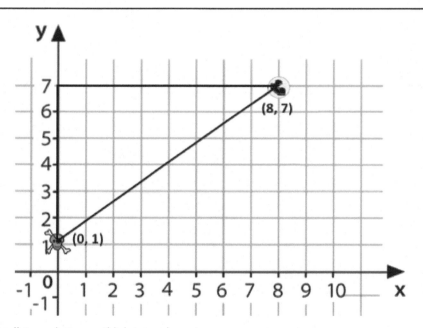

Now write the code to find the distance between this boot and pyret.

_____

_____

_____

The distance between x_1 and x_2 is computed by (`line-length x1 x2`). The distance between y_1 and y_2 is computed by (`line-length y1 y2`). Below is the equation to compute the hypotenuse of a right triangle with those amount for legs:

$$\sqrt{line\text{-}length(x_2, x_1)^2 + line\text{-}length(y_2, y_1)^2}$$

Suppose your player is at **(0, 2)** and a character is at **(4, 5)**. What is the distance between them?

1. Identify the values of x_1, y_1, x_2, and y_2

$x1$	$y1$	$x2$	$y2$
(x-value of 1st point)	*(y-value of 1st point)*	*(x-value of 2nd point)*	*(y-value of 2nd point)*

The equation to compute the distance between these points is:

$$\sqrt{line\text{-}length(4, 0)^2 + line\text{-}length(5, 2)^2}$$

2. Translate the expression above, for (0,2) and (4,5) into a Circle of Evaluation below.

Hint: In our programming language `sqr` *is used for* x^2 *and* `sqrt` *is used for* $\sqrt{x}$

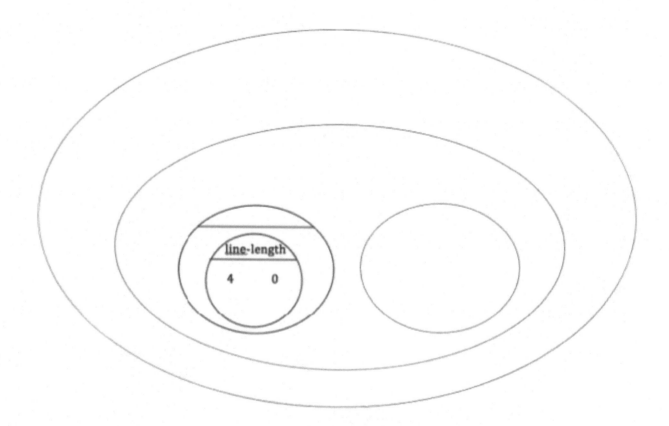

3. Convert the Circle of Evaluation to Code below.

_____

_____

Circle of Evaluation

Computed distance between (1, 3) and (5, 0)

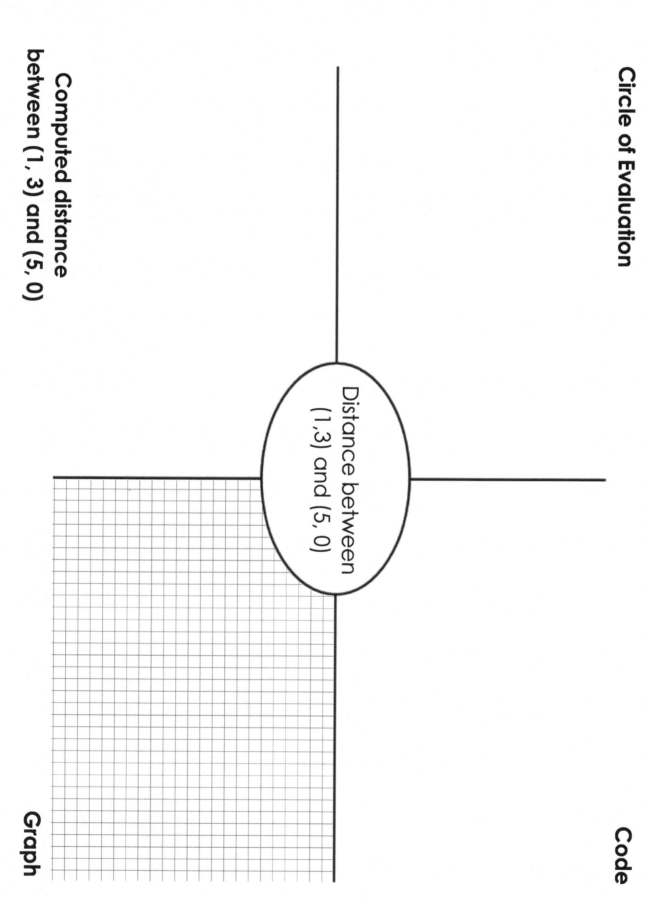

Distance between (1,3) and (5, 0)

Code

Graph

Distance From Game Coordinates

For each of the game screenshots, write the code to calculate the distance between the indicated characters. *The first one has been done for you.*

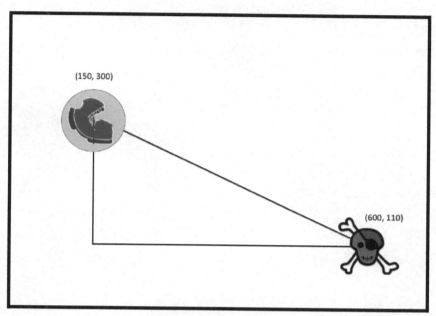

```
(sqrt (+ (sqr (line-length 600 150)) (sqr (line-length 110 300))))
```

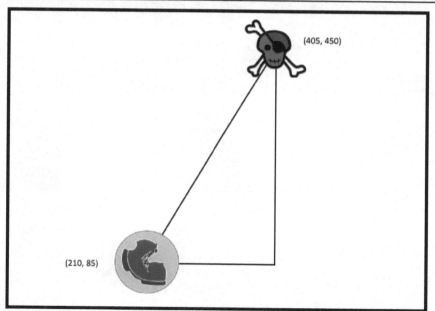

_____

_____

Distance (px, py) to (cx, cy)

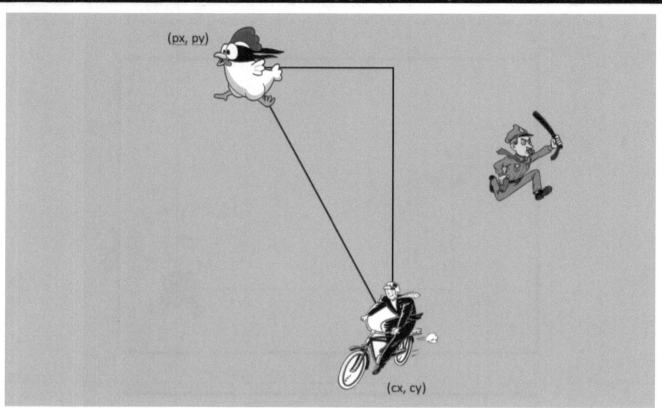

Directions: Use the Design Recipe to write a function `distance`, which takes in FOUR inputs: `px` and `py` (the x- and y-coordinate of the Player) and `cx` and `cy` (the x- and y-coordinates of another character), and produces the distance between them in pixels.

Contract and Purpose Statement

Every contract has three parts…

:

: _____ : _____ -> _____

        function name   *Domain*   *Range*

:

: _____

                           what does the function do?

Examples

Write some examples, then circle and label what changes…

(EXAMPLE (_____) _____)

               function name   *input(s)*   *what the function produces*

(EXAMPLE (_____) _____)

               function name   *input(s)*   *what the function produces*

Definition

Write the definition, giving variable names to all your input values…

(define (_____)

               function name   *variable(s)*

_____)

                       what the function does with those variable(s)

Comparing Code: Finding Missing Distances

For each of the game screenshots below, the math and the code for computing the covered distance is shown. Notice what is similar and what is different about how the top and bottom distances are calculated. Think about why those similarities and differences exist and record your thinking.

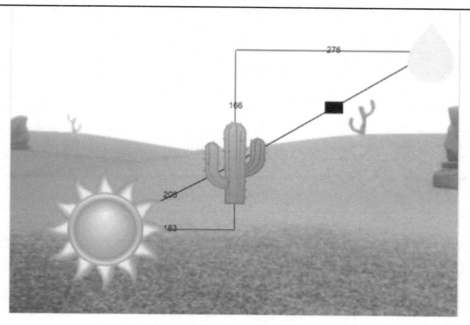

$$\sqrt{166^2 + 276^2}$$

`(sqrt (+ (sqr 166) (sqr 276)))`

$$\sqrt{276^2 - 194^2}$$

`(sqrt (- (sqr 276) (sqr 194)))`

Top Down / Bottom Up

A retractable flag pole starts out 24 inches tall, and grows taller at a rate of 0.6in/sec. An elastic is anchored 200 inches from the base and attached to the top of the pole, forming a right triangle. Using a top-down or bottom-up strategy, define functions that compute the *height* of the pole and the *area* of the triangle after a given number of seconds.

height(sec) = ?
area(sec) = ?

200"
24"

; _____ : _____ -> _____

; _____

(EXAMPLE (_____) _____)

(EXAMPLE (_____) _____)

(define (_____)

_____)

; _____ : _____ -> _____

; _____

(EXAMPLE (_____) _____)

(EXAMPLE (_____) _____)

(define (_____)

_____)

Word Problem: collision?

Directions: Use the Design Recipe to write a function `collision?`, which takes in FOUR inputs: `px` and `py` (the x- and y-coordinate of the Player) and `cx` and `cy` (the x- and y-coordinates of another character), and checks if they are close enough to collide.

Contract and Purpose Statement

Every contract has three parts...

; _____ : _____ -> _____
      function name   *Domain*   *Range*

; _____
                        what does the function do?

Examples

Write some examples, then circle and label what changes...

(EXAMPLE (_____) _____)
             function name   *input(s)*   *what the function produces*

(EXAMPLE (_____) _____)
             function name   *input(s)*   *what the function produces*

Definition

Write the definition, giving variable names to all your input values...

(define (_____)
            function name   *variable(s)*

_____)
                 what the function does with those variable(s)

Contracts

Contracts tell us how to use a function. e.g. `ellipse :: ` **Number**`, ` **Number**`, ` **String**`, ` **String** `-> ` **Image** tells us that the name of the function is `ellipse`, and that it takes four inputs (two Numbers and two Strings). From the contract, we know `(ellipse 100 50 "outline" "red")` will evaluate to an Image.

Name	Domain			Range
`;` `+`	`::`	**Number**`, ` **Number**	`->`	**Number**
`(+ 3 2)`				
`;` `-`	`::`	`Number, Number`	`->`	`Number`
`(- 5 3)`				
`;` `*`	`::`	`Number, Number`	`->`	`Number`
`(* 2 4)`				
`;` `/`	`::`	`Number, Number`	`->`	`Number`
`(/ 8 2)`				
`;` `sqrt`	`::`	`Number`	`->`	`Number`
`(sqrt 25)`				
`;` `sqr`	`::`	`Number`	`->`	`Number`
`(sqr 5)`				
`;` `string-length`	`::`	`String`	`->`	`Number`
`(string-length "Rainbow")`				
`;` `<`	`::`	`Number, Number`	`->`	`Boolean`
`(< 3 2)`				
`;` `>`	`::`	`Number, Number`	`->`	`Boolean`
`(> 3 2)`				

Contracts

Contracts tell us how to use a function. e.g. `ellipse :: Number, Number, String, String -> Image` tells us that the name of the function is `ellipse`, and that it takes four inputs (two Numbers and two Strings). From the contract, we know `(ellipse 100 50 "outline" "fuchsia")` will evaluate to an Image.

Name		Domain		Range
`; =`	`::`	`Number, Number`	`->`	`Boolean`
`(= 3 2)`				
`; <=`	`::`	`Number, Number`	`->`	`Boolean`
`(<= 3 2)`				
`; >=`	`::`	`Number, Number`	`->`	`Boolean`
`(>= 3 2)`				
`; <>`	`::`	`Number, Number`	`->`	`Boolean`
`(<> 3 2)`				
`; string=?`	`::`	`String, String`	`->`	`Boolean`
`(string=? "cat" "kitten")`				
`; string>=?`	`::`	`String, String`	`->`	`Boolean`
`(string>=? "ape" "zebra")`				
`; string<=?`	`::`	`String, String`	`->`	`Boolean`
`(string<=? "Abena" "Zoe")`				
`; string<>?`	`::`	`String, String`	`->`	`Boolean`
`(string<>? "crab" "crawfish")`				
`; string-append`	`::`	`String, String`	`->`	`String`
`(string-append "sun" "shine")`				

Contracts

Contracts tell us how to use a function. e.g. `ellipse :: Number, Number, String, String -> Image` tells us that the name of the function is `ellipse`, and that it takes four inputs (two Numbers and two Strings). From the contract, we know `(ellipse 100 50 "outline" "teal")` will evaluate to an Image.

Name	Domain		Range
; triangle	::	Number, String, Sting	-> Image
(triangle 80 "solid" "green")			
; star	::		->
; circle	::		->
; square	::		->
; rectangle	::		->
; text	::		->
; ellipse	::		->
; regular-polygon	::		->
; rhombus	::		->

Contracts

Contracts tell us how to use a function. e.g. `ellipse :: Number, Number, String, String -> Image` tells us that the name of the function is `ellipse`, and that it takes four inputs (two Numbers and two Strings). From the contract, we know `(ellipse 100 50 "solid" "darkgreen")` will evaluate to an Image.

Name	Domain		Range
; right-triangle	::		->
; isosceles-triangle	::		->
; radial-star	::		->
; star-polygon	::		->
; triangle/sas	::		->
; triangle/asa	::		->
; image-url	::		->
(image-url "https://www.bootstrapworld.org/images/icon.png")			
; scale	::		->
; rotate	::		->

Contracts

Contracts tell us how to use a function. e.g. `ellipse :: Number, Number, String, String -> Image` tells us that the name of the function is `ellipse`, and that it takes four inputs (two Numbers and two Strings). From the contract, we know `(ellipse 100 50 "solid" "lightblue")` will evaluate to an Image.

Name	Domain		Range
; overlay	::	->	
; put-image	::	->	
; flip-horizontal	::	->	
; flip-vertical	::	->	
		->	
; above	::	->	
; beside	::	->	
; or	::	->	
; and	::	->	Boolean
;	::	->	
;		->	